W9-DGA-280

Postcards From The Past

EDWARDIAN IMAGES OF GREATER VANCOUVER AND THE FRASER VALLEY

FRED THIRKELL AND BOB SCULLION

HERITAGE HOUSE

Copyright 1996 Fred Thirkell and Robert Scullion

No part of this publication may be reproduced, stored in a retrieval system, or transmitted in any form or by any means, electronic, mechanical photocopying, recording or otherwise, without the prior written permission of Heritage House Publishing Company Limited.

Canadian Cataloguing in Publication Data

Thirkell, Fred, 1930-
  Postcards from the past

  Includes bibliographical references and index.
  ISBN 1-895811-23-6

  1. Vancouver Metropolitan Area (B.C.)—History—Pictorial works.
2. Fraser River Valley (B.C.)—History—Pictorial works.
3. Postcards—British Columbia—Vancouver Metropolitan Area.
4. Postcards—British Columbia—Fraser River Valley.
I. Scullion, Robert, 1937- II. Title.
FC3847.37.T54 1996   971.1'3303'0222   C96-910554-1
F1089.5.V22T54 1996

First Edition 1996

Heritage House wishes to acknowledge the ongoing support its publishing program receives from Heritage Canada, the Cultural Services Branch of the BC Government and the BC Heritage Trust.

Edited by Joanne Richardson
Interior Design by Robert Scullion and Cecilia Hirczy Welsford
Cover Design, maps and typesetting by Cecilia Hirczy Welsford

Heritage House Publishing Company Limited
#8 – 17921 55th Avenue, Surrey BC V7S 6C4

Printed in Canada

Acknowledgments

Readers may be forgiven if by now they think of "acknowledgments" as little more than obligatory formalities. But they are much more than that: they give credit where credit is due.

Every effort has been made to verify the facts presented. While it was felt that footnotes would be an intrusion, a full bibliography has been included. Peggy Imredy has generously shared her special knowledge of all things pertaining to Stanley Park, and Brian Kelly has provided information regarding the history of the BC Electric Company in the Lower Mainland. Initial encouragement and practical advice regarding the reproduction of old pictures came from Ron Harrison and John Luccock. A special "thank you" goes to all these people.

There is just no way a book about early Vancouver and environs could be researched without the help of archivists and librarians. Staff at the History Desk of the Main Branch of the Vancouver Public Library and at the Reference Desk of the New Westminster Public Library were always more than willing to facilitate research. Robin Inglis and June Thompson of the North Vancouver Archives, Valerie Francis of the New Westminster Museum, Valerie Billesberger and her staff at the Mission Community Archives, and Kris Foulds of the Abbotsford Archives (MSA Museum Society) provided much appreciated help with research relating to the history of their respective communities

If any part of these acknowledgments should be printed in bold letters, it would stress the assistance provided by the staff of the Vancouver City Archives. Their knowledge of the Matthews Collection and City Records saved us many hours of work. The assistance provided by Sue Baptie (city archivist), Carol Haber, Donna MacKinnon, Elaine Burton, and Ann Carroll was appreciated beyond words. They are very special people, indeed.

And speaking of very special people, the critical advice offered at home was gratefully, if not always gracefully, received! Lil Thirkell laboured to keep Fred from using a hundred words where twenty would suffice, and Beth Fish not only proofread Bob's final draft but, like Lil, made valuable suggestions along the way.

PREFACE

Our selection of eighty-four lithographed postcards combine to offer a unique perspective on Vancouver and the Lower Mainland. There are three predominant reasons why.

We have focused on the years between 1901 and 1910. These Edwardian years were boom years in Vancouver. It was a vibrant time when optimism was infectious and people believed that, every day in every way, life was getting better and better. This positive mood was reflected both in the physical growth of the city and in the first redevelopment of the downtown area.

Second, we have used a neglected but unique pictorial record to illustrate Vancouver's past – a record provided by lithographed or printed picture postcards produced before the First World War. A significant percentage of the pictures used in this book will not be found in any public archival collection.

Our third reason for producing *Postcards From The Past: Edwardian Images of Greater Vancouver and the Fraser Valley* has to do with pleasure – our pleasure in researching, compiling, and presenting the material and, we hope, your pleasure in reading about and viewing pictures produced during the years when Vancouver came of age as a city.

For those who might like to see the buildings that still stand, or the sites where those that have been razed once stood, see the maps on pages 10 and 11.

As the Edwardian era approaches its centennial, this book is our contribution in celebration of a unique period in Vancouver's past.

Fred Thirkell and Bob Scullion

TABLE OF CONTENTS

INTRODUCTION

Postcards *From The Past* has been subtitled *Edwardian Images* for good reason. The period it covers approximates the years of Edward VII's reign. Edward had been Prince of Wales for sixty years when he succeeded Queen Victoria, his mother, to the throne in 1901. Both Edward and his people lived through the sober-sided society of Queen Victoria's declining years. He did not, however, share his mother's sombre perspective. In fact, early in his life, he learned how attractive beauty and pleasure could be. When he became king, it was as though the whole British Empire had at last been given permission to enjoy the gifts that life had to offer.

Another thing that King Edward discovered, to his profit, during his decades as Prince of Wales was that people who made money could be both interesting and useful. Queen Elizabeth's private fortune is largely built on the investments her great grandfather made, based on the advice of the financiers in his circle. Queen Victoria and Prince Albert believed that one's station in life was determined by birth alone. While they appreciated accomplishment in people from all levels of society, they firmly believed that those not well-born could never achieve significant social advancement. Edward, however, had no problem at all with people "getting ahead." And that was exactly what everyone was trying to do, even on the edge of the Empire in far-off Vancouver!

While this book is not intended to be a social history, certain things can be said about Vancouverites in the Edwardian years. First of all, just about everyone was a newcomer, and people, therefore, pretty much had to take each other at face value. *What* you were was much more important than *who* you were. There was a certain egalitarianism that suggested one person was as good as the next and had a right to try to make it to the top. The song whose lines included "I danced with the man, who danced with the girl, who danced with the Prince of Wales" summed up popular social attitudes.

Egalitarianism only went so far, though. The reality was that people of money were also people of position. From there, a certain leap in logic brought popular thinking to the conclusion that those of position were by definition men and women of character. Vancouverites were not unique in this assumption, however. Even the Canadian Immigration Department regulations required that "as soon as a vessel reaches a Canadian port, the second and third-class passengers have to appear before the immigration officials, and reply to sundry questions as to the amount of money they possess and what they propose to do in the country. First class passengers are exempt from this examination."

The years of King Edward's reign, 1901–1910, bracketed Vancouver's coming of age. The city was twenty-one years old in 1907, and just as human beings experience all sorts of change in their early adult years, so do cities. Words that come to mind in connection with growing up are "impetuous," "testing," and even "rash." The *Oxford Universal Dictionary* tells us that rash means "acting without due consideration of regard for consequences, undue haste, want of consideration." These three words could be used to describe Vancouver in the years before the depression of 1912–13 and the First World War brought the city's era of youthful exuberance to a sudden and unexpected end.

VANCOUVER'S GROWTH

What about the city's growth during the Edwardian years? In round figures Vancouver, a town of 27,000 in 1901, grew to a city of nearly 121,000 by 1911. The value of building permits issued went from $833,607 in 1902 to $19,388,322 in 1912. The 1912 figure was only exceeded once – in 1929 – before the end of the Second World War, when Vancouver's growth again took off. In December 1912, only Chicago and New York had a greater dollar value for building permits than did Vancouver and Philadelphia, the two cities that were virtually tied for third place in North America.

The face of Vancouver was rapidly and radically changed by its phenomenal growth in population. Between 1900 and 1912, for example, twenty-five new schools were built, and three existing ones were significantly enlarged. New schools were also built in the neighbouring municipalities of Vancouver South and Point Grey. The court house built in 1890 was inadequate by 1906, and an annex for the new building that was to replace it was on the drawing board before the new court house was opened in 1911. The stone post office built in the 1890s at the corner of Granville and Pender was replaced by a larger building at Granville and Hastings in 1910.

Commercial development also boomed. The Dominion Trust Building opened in 1910 as the Empire's tallest, only to have its title taken away from it by the World (later Sun) Tower in 1912. But all was not sunshine. In the years before the Great War, real estate was over-promoted, if not actually manipulated, by the army of realtors, speculators, and "capitalists " who bought and sold property in the rapidly expanding city. Interestingly, if they could justify appropriating the title, businessmen proudly listed their occupation as "capitalist" in the directories of those long-gone halcyon days.

Even today, in Vancouver the words "real estate manipulation" evoke old stories of the CPR (Canadian Pacific Railway). The railway naturally did all it could to maximize the financial return on its land holdings. It pulled the centre of the city west from Hastings and Main Streets to Granville and Georgia Streets, thereby making its West End lands both more valuable and more marketable. While it can never be known with certainty, had the CPR not redefined the city to its advantage, it is probable another consortium would have moved in to do so. Developers looking for opportunities to make money, particularly where municipal regulation is lax or non-existent, is not a new phenomenon.

As it happened, even the CPR hadn't anticipated the speed at which Vancouver would grow. Its first Hotel Vancouver, opened in 1887, had to be enlarged three times before the second Hotel Vancouver was opened in 1916. Its train station had to be replaced twice before 1914, and its wharves and docks were still being extended when war broke out in August 1914, just before the new Pier D was completed.

The pictures that make up this book attempt to recapture the face of Vancouver and its surrounding communities in the Edwardian years. Many of the buildings pictured existed for only a relatively short time – twenty or thirty years in some instances – and therefore can only be revisited through photographs. The pictures used are the lithographed postcards that were so popular in the Edwardian era.

THE FIRST POSTCARDS

It was Heinrich von Stephan, a German postal official (later the German Empire's postmaster general), who first suggested the idea of an *offenes Postblatt* or "open mailpage." He presented the idea to an Austro-German postal conference in Karlsruhe in 1865. The "mailpage" would bear an imprinted stamp at a rate significantly below the letter rate. The idea was rejected out of fear that postal income would be drastically reduced. On January 26, 1869, Dr. Emmanuel Herrmann, a professor of political science at the military academy in Vienna, published an article in the influential Viennese *Neue Freie Presse,* in which he argued that there would be great economic advantage to the Treasury from the introduction of the *Correspondenz-Karte* or *Postkarte*.

Herrmann's argument won the day in Vienna. Baron von Maly, the postmaster general, was convinced, and on October 1, 1869, the world's first postcards went on sale throughout the Austro-Hungarian Empire. The imprinted two-kreuzer stamp bore the image of Emperor Franz Joseph in the upper right corner of that side of the postcard that provided three dotted lines for the name and address of the recipient. On the back was space for a message as well as a note in small print absolving the Imperial postal service of any responsibility for the contents of the message.

The cards were an immediate success, and more than nine million were sold in the first year. Ironically, the introduction of the *Correspondenz-Karte,* as it was officially called, was greeted as a victory for democracy. With the reduction in the cost of postage, the postcard extended the use of the postal service to every level of society. Until the introduction of the *Correspondenz-Karte,* the price of postage was dictated by the distance the letter had to travel and by the number of sheets it contained.

Soon many countries were issuing postcards. Prince Bismark authorized the first German *Correspondenz-Karte* on July 1, 1870; Great Britain followed suit on October 1, 1870; and Canada got on the bandwagon in 1871. The Canadian card could be posted for one cent within city limits and for two cents outside city limits. While Canada introduced postcards on July 1, 1871, the United States didn't permit their use at a reduced postal rate until May 13, 1873. The 1886 World Congress of the Universal Postal Union meeting in Lisbon sanctioned the international use of postcards. And all this enthusiasm was for post office-issued cards that were without pictures!

PICTURE POSTCARDS

While there is no difficulty in knowing the exact date when the world's first government-issued postcard appeared, or when a particular country introduced postcards as postal stationery, it is not so easy to say where and when the first *picture* postcard was produced. One early commercially produced card came into being during the Franco-Prussian War. It was the work of M. Léon Bésnardeau, a bookseller from the French village of Sillé-la-Guillaume. There were 40,000 French troops, most of whom had minimal education, stationed nearby at Conlie. He reasoned that these men would want to send messages home and would welcome a means of so doing that didn't involve laboriously producing a letter. He was right! He had his cards printed in November 1870 and almost immediately had to go to a second printing. His cards included lithographs of military emblems and patriotic allegories. These pictorials were what made Bésnardeau's cards unique, and they support his claim to have published the first picture postcard. However, the fact that the cards had to be mailed at full letter rate fuels the debate as to whether or not Bésnardeau's cards were, indeed, the world's first bona fide picture postcards.

Also, in late 1870 a British lithographer, John S. Day, offered a postcard for sale. It was printed on the back of the official half-penny postcard and featured a *coloured* decorative frame of holly and mistletoe encircling the words "good wishes." Day's card was the first coloured postcard and the progenitor of generations of greeting postcards produced for every occasion from Christmas and Easter to Halloween and Ground Hog Day.

On May 1, 1882, Ludwig Zrenner produced a postcard to mark the opening of the Nuremberg Exhibition. On it appears a lithograph of the exhibition grounds' entrance gate. It is claimed that this is the first postcard to display a picture produced from a photograph. Regardless of whether in fact the card was the world's first *picture* postcard, it was the first of a long line of cards produced to commemorate special events. There were a number of other cards that claimed to have been the world's first *picture* postcard, and each claimant has its champions. In the final analysis, though, the title cannot be awarded unconditionally to any one claimant.

FURTHER DEVELOPMENTS

It was the Paris Exhibition of 1889 that launched picture postcards on their campaign to conquer the world. A card picturing the new Eiffel Tower could be purchased, stamped, and posted from the top of the 984-foot edifice. Britain copied the idea in 1891 by producing a card on the reverse side of an official postcard for the Royal Naval Exhibition.

This card pictured the Eddystone lighthouse. The British government finally gave up its monopoly on the production of postcards on September 1, 1894, when it allowed the production of private postcards (to which could be affixed the half-penny stamp).

It was the beginning of the twentieth century before postcards with "divided backs" came into being. Until then, the picture and the message shared one side of the card, while the postage stamp and mailing address took up the other side. There were, however, some exceptions. Some countries had allowed pictorial vignettes to appear on the front of the cards, provided there was sufficient space for the stamp and the address. Great Britain permitted "divided backs" in 1902, and Canada allowed them on December 18, 1903. While the Universal Postal Union approved them in 1906, the United States did not permit their use until March 1, 1907. The advent of the divided back, which provided space for both message and address, meant that the opposite side could be completely occupied by a picture. In other words, the picture postcard as we know it had been born.

POSTCARDS AND VANCOUVER

It is hard to appreciate the popularity of the picture postcard in the Edwardian era. Before the First World War it seemed as though *everyone* was sending, receiving, and collecting postcards. In Germany, some 1.1 billion went through the post in 1903. Here in Canada, in 1910 over seven million people mailed over forty-five million postcards. And in the same year in British Columbia, with its population of 407,000, over 2.7 million postcards were mailed. As well, of course, countless cards were bought by locals and tourists alike for their respective postcard albums.

What about subject matter? Views of Stanley Park outsold all others. Also popular were natural wonders such as Capilano Canyon, the Lions, and the First Narrows. The Edwardians, true to their times, though, were equally excited by the latest, largest, and most impressive of man-made wonders. A view of the First Narrows, for example, was better if the *Empress of India* or some other ocean liner was passing by. They happily bought postcards proving that far-off Vancouver was both civilized and a city to write home about.

This book contains a sampling of eighty-four lithographed cards, dating primarily from 1901 to 1910. The cards selected were all originally produced in black and white. While there are plenty of coloured lithographs available from this period, these were traditionally touched up to the point where they lost any resemblance to reality. In them, electric wires, streetcar tracks, unpaved roads, and other "unsightly" elements were often removed. By and large, black and white lithographs escaped the hand of the touch-up artist. And why lithographs rather than photographs?

First, Edwardians were likely to buy lithographed cards rather than photo cards simply because of cost; a lithographed card cost a penny, while a postcard produced from a photograph could cost anywhere from two to five cents. Second, lithographed cards, because they were cheaper to produce, were generally published in larger numbers than were photographically produced cards. This, in turn, meant the subject matter needed to have a wide appeal. Third, in British Columbia lithographs, and their importance as a visual historical record, have been neglected.

Perhaps their huge success was their undoing. Could anything as common as a printed postcard have anything of value to say? Some of the cards, like those in this book, have become relatively rare. While postcards were produced in the thousands, they were also destroyed in the thousands. There is a final reason why this book centres on black and white printed postcards: the two who created it think they are great!

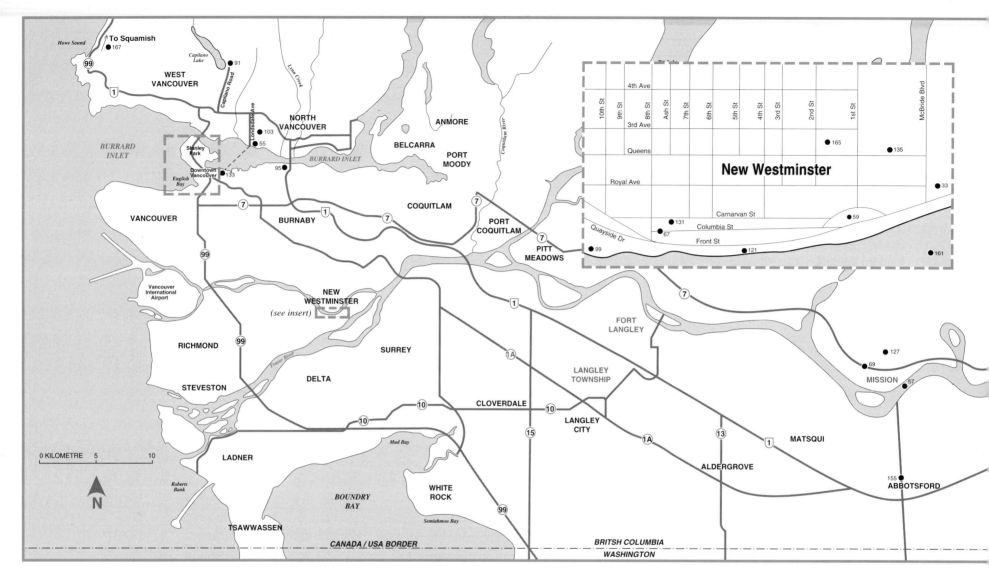

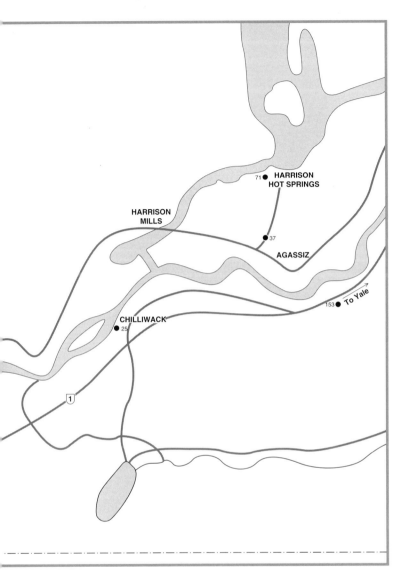

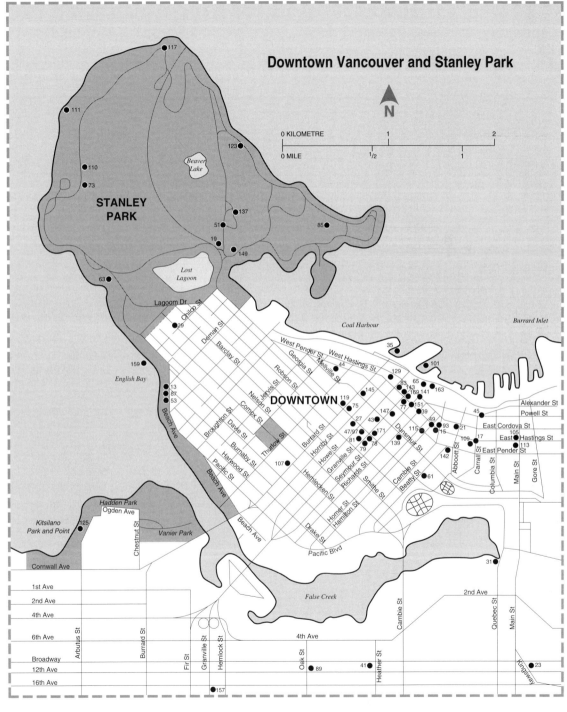

HARRISON HOT SPRINGS 71

HARRISON MILLS

AGASSIZ

37

CHILLIWACK

25

153 To Yale

1

Downtown Vancouver and Stanley Park

N

0 KILOMETRE   1   2

0 MILE   1/2   1

STANLEY PARK

Beaver Lake

Lost Lagoon

English Bay

Coal Harbour

Burrard Inlet

DOWNTOWN

Lagoon Dr.

Chilco St

Denman St

Barclay St

West Pender St

West Hastings St

Melville St

Georgia St

Robson St

Jervis St

Nelson St

Comox St

Broughton St

Davie St

Burnaby St

Harwood St

Pacific St

Beach Ave

Beach Ave

Thurlow St

Burrard St

Hornby St

Howe St

Granville St

Seymour St

Richards St

Homer St

Hamilton St

Smithe St

Cambie St

Beatty St

Drake St

Hemlocken St

Abbott St

Carrall St

Columbia St

Main St

Gore St

Alexander St

Powell St

East Cordova St

East Hastings St

East Pender St

Hadden Park

Ogden Ave

Kitsilano Park and Point

Chestnut St

Vanier Park

Cornwall Ave

False Creek

1st Ave

2nd Ave

4th Ave

6th Ave

Broadway

12th Ave

16th Ave

Arbutus St

Burrard St

Fir St

Granville St

Hemlock St

Oak St

Heather St

Cambie St

Quebec St

Main St

Kingsway

2nd Ave

4th Ave

Pacific Blvd

WATCH THE BIRDIE

While the spectators' attention is focused on the row-boat races at English Bay, the photographer on the edge of the crowded scene is focusing on them. Even though there are literally hundreds of thousands of different postcards, there are very few that include pictures of postcard photographers in action. This picture, printed by T.N. Hibben and Company of Victoria, has, therefore, a special significance for both photo buffs and postcard collectors alike.

There is no way of knowing whether the photographer is a professional or an amateur. The so-called postcard camera was very popular at the turn of the century, and many people owned one. Even today, a great many families will have in their albums postcard-sized pictures of parents or grandparents taken years ago by some family member who "dabbled in photography." The backs of these photographs will be the same as those found on the commercially sold postcards of the day.

Commercially produced postcards appeared in a variety of shapes and sizes. Some were elongated to 3½-by-8½ inches, some were "miniatures" of 2¾-by-4½ inches, and still others were produced in a bookmark format. While there were a variety of cards produced in novelty sizes, the majority adopted the standard 3½-by-5½ inch postcard size.

On occasion, exactly the same view would be published as (1) a photograph, (2) a black and white lithograph, and (3) a coloured lithograph. Generally speaking, the card began life as a photo postcard produced and marketed by a local studio. Large national or international firms were not likely to risk producing cards that might have only limited appeal. However, should it happen that a locally produced photo card had wide general appeal, a major publisher of postcards might arrange to buy the rights to its production and put it on the market as a photo card, a lithographed black and white card, or a coloured printed card. When this happened, the company's name would invariably appear on the back of the card.

As in any line of business, there were some publishers who were less than scrupulous. Unfortunately, pirating of pictures was not uncommon. Sooner or later – and more probably sooner – anyone who collects postcards will come across anonymously printed cards that reproduce local photo cards already in his or her collection. When there is no publisher's name on the back of a card, it can be assumed the picture has been pirated from some local commercial photographer. The original postcard will invariably carry the name of the individual or firm that first produced it.

Returning to our picture, it was taken sometime between 1904 and 1906. One not only wonders who the photographer was, but who it was who took *his* picture on that sunny summers's afternoon at English Bay.

VANCOUVER'S FIRST PERMANENT COURT HOUSE

Records indicate that there was a small lock-up and court room in the village of Granville in the early 1870s. This structure was replaced in 1883 by a 22-by-26-foot building on Water Street. Like the rest of Vancouver it went up in smoke on June 13, 1886. Various rented quarters, including Sullivan's Hall, were used for the court until the fall of 1890, when the city's first permanent court house opened. The new building on Pender Street was at the top side of what was then Government Square, later Victory Square.

Designed by Thomas Sorby and built by Turnbull and Company of New Westminster at a cost of $17,996, the court house was vaguely Georgian in style. On its upper floor was a court room, judge's room, and the law library. The lower floor had space for the county registrar, the timber inspector, the assessor, and a janitor. When the building was opened, a banquet, which went on long past midnight, was held in the court room. The following day a *Daily News-Advertiser* reporter told the court registrar, who later retold the story, that "on returning to his office with copy about 4:00 AM he saw the Court House fully lighted and on entering the Court Room saw in the middle of the floor, the tables arranged in a horseshoe, with the janitor stretched out dead to the world on a bier of empty bottles." A Victorian sense of propriety and an awe of the judiciary doubtless kept the reporter from even considering filing his story for printing in the next day's paper.

Even while the building was under construction, its limited size was questioned. A.E. Beck, the court registrar, had suggested to Sorby that the accommodation would soon prove inadequate. Sorby replied that the building would be larger than the court house at Chilliwack, a much older place. And who could argue with such logic? Within two years the Vancouver Court House was, in fact, too small, and plans had to be developed for an addition three or four times larger than the original building. Excavation began on March 9, 1883. Designed by N.E. Hoffar and built by J.M. McLuckie and Edward Cook at a cost of $46,954, the addition dwarfed the original building. It had both style and a lot of steps, as our picture shows. Its outstanding feature was a raised cupola surmounted by a statue of Justice.

The building was torn down after the new court house on Georgia Street opened in 1911. However, there is one remaining legacy from the days when Victory Square was Government Square – the maple trees. Beck, who was not only court registrar but government agent, was responsible for having the grounds landscaped. Since the government wouldn't give him any money for the beautification of the grounds, on his own initiative he contacted the Dominion Experimental Farm at Agassiz and scrounged trees and shrubs. He paid a dollar per tree to get the thirty maple trees planted. Mr. Justice Irving later offered Beck the gift of an ornamental fountain for Government Square, but the government declined to accept: the cost of maintaining the fountain was considered to be, in Beck's words, "too great a charge on the King's Revenue." How times have changed!

CARRALL AND HASTINGS

Looking at the corner of Carrall and Hastings today it is hard to believe that before the First World War this intersection was at the heart of Vancouver. Within a two-block radius were theatres like the Bijou and Pantages, hotels like the Europe and Woods, and businesses of all descriptions. Two blocks west was the court house, two blocks east was the public library, two blocks north was the waterfront (with its endless activity), and at the centre of it all stood the BC Electric Railway Company's tram station. Throughout its years of existence the BC Electric Railway Company was commonly referred to simply as the BC Electric.

Pictured on the right is the city's first interurban station. It was a two-storey brick building erected at a cost of $24,000. It served as both a terminus for the New Westminster and Vancouver Tramway and as the BC Electric's head office. Considering its less than inspired architecture, it may come as a surprise to learn that this unprepossessing building was designed by none other than Francis Rattenbury, BC's most celebrated architect. The building was torn down in March of 1911 to make way for a much larger and more elegant station and head office.

Just beyond the BC Electric's building can be seen the turret and part of the illuminated sign belonging to the Woods Hotel, which still stands on the southeast corner of Carrall and Hastings. The hostelry advertised 90 rooms, 20 baths, 10 fire exits, an elevator service, and a dining room that could accommodate 75 guests. Across the street, on the northeast corner, was a variety of shops, above which were the offices of "The Chicago Dentists." They doubtless competed for suffering patients with "The Boston Dentists," located four blocks west on Hastings. These dental partnerships coupled local dentists with syndicates that supplied them with advertising, equipment, and updated technical information.

Right in the middle of the picture are the CPR train tracks cutting diagonally across Hastings Street. The tracks connected the railway's Burrard Inlet waterfront station with its yards, shops, and roundhouse (now part of a local community centre on False Creek). A number of times a day for fifty-five years Hastings Street traffic was held up while empty passenger coaches were moved to and from the yards. July 17, 1932, was a day for celebrating: the railway's much-awaited 1.6-mile-long tunnel connecting the station to the yards was put into operation, and, to the joy of all, the tracks running across Hastings were no longer needed. Part of the old CPR right-of-way is now Pigeon Park. Interestingly, the tunnel that replaced the street-level crossing is, itself, no longer used by the railway. Following reconstruction, this tunnel is now part of SkyTrains's route to its downtown Vancouver terminus, located at the former CPR station on Cordova Street.

COLONEL MOODY AND STANLEY PARK

While Lord Strathcona may have named Stanley Park on September 1, 1888, and Mayor Oppenheimer may have opened it on September 27, 1888, and Lord Stanley himself may have dedicated it on October 29, 1889, it was really Colonel Richard Moody, Chief Commissioner of Lands and Works for the Colony of British Columbia, who was most responsible for the park that quickly became Vancouver's pride and joy. His "gift" was quite unintentional, of course.

In 1863 Colonel Moody set aside the 950-acre peninsula as a military reserve. In so doing, he saved what was later to become Stanley Park from the many get-rich-quick entrepreneurs who infested the new city of Vancouver in the late 1880s. Had the acreage not been reserved, it undoubtedly would have been logged, subdivided, and lost forever as parkland.

In 1886, Vancouver's first city council petitioned the federal government, asking that the land be given to the city as a park. The request was acceded to by an order-in-council provided the city "keep the park in order and the dominion government retain the right to resume the property at any time." The government also insisted that the tract's "natural integrity" should be disturbed as little as possible. From a military point of view a forested site would be of much greater use as a point of defence than would logged-off acreage.

In 1887, anticipating that the park would be theirs, voters agreed to spend $20,000 on landscaping and on building a road around it. At the same time, city council authorized the building of a bridge across Coal Harbour in order to make the park more accessible. The next year it appointed Henry Avison as the city's first park ranger, at a salary of sixty dollars a month.

Our picture is taken from the Coal Harbour bridge and looks towards the park ranger's lodge. This cottage was built at a cost of $458 by F. Young to the design of E. Mallondaise. The nearby stable cost an additional ninety-eight dollars. On April 13, 1891, the newly created Vancouver Parks Board felt moved to spend $36.55 for a uniform, helmet, and badge for Mr. Avison to wear on Sundays and holidays. One particular entry in the minutes suggests that the Parks Board was always very business-like. At its meeting of August 8, 1896, it was reported that "Henry Avison had ceased to act in the capacity of Park Ranger since July 31, and that consequently his name was taken off the pay sheet." This was the Parks Board's way of saying that the poor fellow had died!

In 1904, when George Eldon had the job, the title of park ranger was changed to superintendent of parks. This title was more appropriate to the individual, who was not only responsible for Stanley Park, but also for a large and growing system of urban parks and playgrounds. Over the years, the Vancouver Parks Board has managed to maintain and expand this magnificent reserve of parklands within the city, a legacy that started with the strategic decision of a military man over 130 years ago.

"For The Better Class Of Tourists"

Vancouver's Hotel Metropole advertised itself in directories of the day as "a favourite resort of the better class of tourists and the travelling public." Opened in 1894, it was designed by R. MacKay Fripp and, architecturally, was very much of its time. It was solidly Victorian, four stories high, and made of brick; it had picturesque turrets and its detailing was vaguely Romanesque. Located on the west side of Abbott, between Hastings and Cordova Streets, it was rated as one of Vancouver's four best hotels in the 1890s. The other three were the Hotel Vancouver at Granville and Georgia, the Badminton at Dunsmuir and Howe, and the Commercial on Cambie between Hastings and Cordova.

By 1908, the Metropole's advertising could boast that every one of its eighty-four rooms had gas *and* electric light as well as hot and cold running water and a telephone. Daily rates in 1908 were "American Plan $2 and up, European Plan $1 and up." A free bus was available to carry guests to and from the boats and trains. The Metropole also claimed to offer "the best cuisine the market affords, served by affable and courteous waiters." The fact that the disposition of the waiters rated special mention may suggest their demeanour had a reputation to the contrary.

The lobby of the Hotel Metropole, pictured here, reflected the popular taste and habits of the Edwardian years. Potted plants in oriental jardinières dressed up the otherwise sparsely furnished area. Fir V-joint wainscotting protected the columns and walls, while a stencilled border surrounded the room just below the ceiling. Mercury, tirelessly standing on one foot throughout the years, adorned the newel post. In all probability his raised hand held some kind of electric lighting fixture. The registration desk and glassed-in manager's office took up one whole side of the lobby. Altogether the decor suggested a masculine space – an impression that was reinforced by the presence of a brass spittoon and a glass cigar display counter. While men might loiter in the lobby, women would have been expected to move rather quickly through this male preserve. After all, there was an elevator that could take them to their own refuge, the Ladies' Parlour, one floor up.

The Metropole's end was brought about by success – not its own, but that of its neighbour, Woodward's Department Store. The hotel was demolished in 1925 to make room for an addition to Woodward's. Its name, however, continues to this day on the other side of Abbott Street, where a somewhat less stylish Hotel Metropole is still open for business.

MOUNT PLEASANT SCHOOL

Captain Stamp's Hastings Mill on Burrard Inlet came into being in 1865. It was not long before a shack town grew up around it, and the need for a school became apparent to the little community that would become Vancouver. The mill donated the necessary lumber for an eighteen-by-forty-foot schoolhouse, and the provincial government was asked to provide a teacher. This it did in the person of Miss Julia Sweeny, daughter of the mill's machinist. The one-room schoolhouse, standing near Hastings Mill on what is now Dunlevy Avenue, opened on February 28, 1872, with fewer than twenty pupils. For a time the building doubled on Sundays as a church for both Anglicans and Methodists.

By 1888 Vancouver's growth required two more schools, both of which opened in November. The school built at Burrard and Barclay in today's West End, then called the West School, became Dawson School in 1893 and finally Aberdeen School in 1907, when a new and much larger Dawson School was built a few blocks away. The other new school was erected at the corner of Westminster Road (now Kingsway) and Ninth Avenue (now Broadway). Known as the False Creek School, it was the only school between False Creek and New Westminster. Quite literally "a little red schoolhouse," it opened with forty-two pupils. The first teacher was Miss A.J. McDougall, who earned the standard salary for a teacher at that time – fifty-five dollars a month.

In 1892 the Vancouver School Board built four new brick eight-room school buildings. One was the city's first high school, and the other three were Dawson, Strathcona – successor to the original Hastings Mill School – and Mount Pleasant. "Mount Pleasant" was the new, more eloquent name for what had been False Creek School. It took its name from the area it served and was at the centre of Vancouver's first residential suburb. The buildings erected in 1892 had a strong family resemblance, and all four may have been designed by Thomas Hooper. The new Mount Pleasant School faced some construction delays and didn't open until 1893. In 1897, Dawson, Strathcona, and Mount Pleasant Schools were each doubled in size to sixteen rooms.

Pictured is the enlarged Mount Pleasant School. Built of brick, with stone decorative trim, the school was very much in the Romanesque Revival style, a style popularized in the eastern United States by H.H. Richardson a generation earlier. As can easily be seen, the eight-room addition was a mirror image of the original building. The school retained its original appearance until it was demolished in the 1970s, when a shopping centre was built on the site. Mount Pleasant School had moved by then into a new building, which is still in use on Guelph Street.

THE RIVERBOAT LANDING

If we were to play a game of word association and say "paddlewheeler," then without a pause someone would come back with "Mississippi." Although Tom Sawyer and Huck Finn, riverboat gamblers and southern belles, to say nothing of countless movies, have made us think of the riverboat as something uniquely American, the fact is that paddlewheelers were more extensively used in British Columbia than in any other part of North America. And why was that? Because, as someone once said, they could sail on damp grass! Because they were flat-bottomed, and generally required little more than a foot of water to float, they were ideally suited to BC's shallow rivers. As well, the fact that they were made of wood meant that they could easily be repaired. They could also be prefabricated, taken to where they could be assembled, and put to work in a matter of days. Two boats, each consisting of over a thousand pieces, were in fact shipped west from Toronto.

In British Columbia, sternwheelers were much more popular than were sidewheelers. Sidewheelers needed wharves for docking, were hard to manage in narrow channels, and their sidewheels got jammed and damaged by river debris. Sternwheelers had none of these problems and, most important, could nose into shore almost anywhere and let down a gangplank.

Riverboats first came to the lower Fraser River in 1858, carrying eager would-be miners to the gold fields. From gold-rush days down through the railway construction years, sternwheelers regularly travelled the 110 miles between New Westminster and Yale. After the completion of the CPR in 1885, they generally ran only as far as Chilliwack and Harrison Mills. While the riverboats would stop virtually anywhere to pick up passengers or freight, they did have regular ports of call, such as Port Hammond, Port Haney, Port Kells, Mission City, and Harrison Mills. Furthermore, on both sides of the river were places like Miller's Landing, Codville Landing, Minto Landing, and Chilliwack Landing, where, as required, ships would stop for mail, passengers, and freight.

Pictured is Chilliwack Landing, which was about two and a half miles from the centre of present-day Chilliwack. Even though it had three stores, a post office, hotel, livery barn, and landing shed, it had little chance of growing. If it wasn't actually on Stó:lõ, land it was certainly surrounded by reserve. Furthermore, the continual erosion of the river bank and the risk of flooding made the landing less than ideal for permanent settlement.

Our picture has a certain serenity about it. Perhaps the sternwheeler has just left, as have most of the people. All we see are a buggy, a covered wagon, and a dray. For whatever reason, their owners are the last to leave the landing on a lazy summer day. Chilliwack Landing and the other ports of call lost most of their importance when the BC Electric Company's interurban line opened in 1910. The *Skeena*, the last riverboat running, was tied up in New Westminster in 1925 when its owner-captain died. The era of the sternwheeler and the riverboat landing on the lower Fraser River was over.

Vancouver's Second Court House

Vancouver's old court house, which stood on what was later to become Victory Square, had long been inadequate by the time Premier McBride's government purchased land for a new court house in August of 1906. A full city block, bounded by Georgia, Howe, Robson, and Hornby Streets, was bought for $46,000. There was considerable objection to the site. Many people felt it was too far from the centre of the city, which was still down along Hastings and Cordova Streets. In the same year, Francis Rattenbury won the design competition for the new building.

Rattenbury chose a Beaux-Arts Neo-Classical style for his court house. Its exterior was given importance by a massive flight of granite steps – guarded by twin lions – leading to an imposing pillared portico. Materials employed were the same as those Rattenbury had used for the Parliament Buildings in Victoria, namely, Nelson Island granite for the first floor and Haddington Island stone for everything else. Rattenbury's specifications for the interior, which centred on a rotunda circled by sixteen Corinthian columns, called for extensive use of marble and fine woods. In fact, he insisted that all materials be of the highest quality throughout and that the workmanship be the finest possible.

Construction began in the autumn of 1907 and was to be completed in two years at a cost of $400,000. As it turned out, the building was not finished until 1911 and was $60,000 over budget. Construction delays and cost overruns are nothing new. One design change was made while the building was under construction, when the powers that be decided that the shallow, copper-sheathed dome was too low to be seen properly from Georgia Street. In response to this, the designers built a temporary wooden mock-up so they could see for themselves how things would look when the work was completed. The wooden mock-up proved its worth, and the square stone podium supporting the dome was raised five feet.

One bizarre incident marked the history of the Vancouver Court House. On November 4, 1942, for reasons still unknown, someone set two dynamite blasts that fractured the rear end of the fifteen-ton west lion. The injury to this symbol of British justice was expertly repaired by two of the men who had carved the beast from Nelson Island granite more than thirty years earlier.

At the official opening of the new court house on October 19, 1911, Attorney-General Bowser announced that it was already too small and that construction would begin immediately on an addition (which became known as the West Wing). Vancouver's population had doubled to 100,000 in the time it took to erect the building, and twice as many people meant twice as many court cases. Rattenbury's court house was replaced in 1979 by a new and larger complex, and the old building was remodelled to become the city's art gallery. As a footnote, it is interesting to know that the land that cost $46,000 and was so far from the centre of things in 1906 had a market value one hundred times that in 1983!

THE WEST END

The West End was Vancouver's most prestigious residential area for most of the city's first quarter century. It all began in 1887, when the CPR put its prime land west of Granville Street on the market. Lots were expensive, but prices from $350 to $1,000 did not discourage buyers. Soon elaborate residences were being built along the tree-lined streets. Brochures promoting Vancouver as a place to live and do business would often use pictures like this one of Nelson Street to lure potential settlers. They always managed to imply, of course, that such streets were typical, the kind one would find anywhere in Vancouver! The Information Bureau's 1907 *Greater Vancouver Illustrated,* for example, said of the city that, "while new, it is not crude... The city is solid, well-built, with architectural display, and everything wears an air of prosperity and permanence." The West End's "prosperity and permanence" was relatively short-lived, however, as a number of factors conspired to bring about the area's decline.

The most severe blow came when the CPR created 250-acre Shaughnessy Heights in 1907. Its name, large lots laid out along crescents that followed the natural contours of its hillside location, and the requirement that any house built must cost at least $6,000 gave the area an immediate appeal to the city's wealthy. Shaughnessy was expensive, but the fact that the rich appreciated being reminded that they were rich had not escaped the attention of the CPR's Land Department. Very soon the city's elite began deserting the West End, moving both physically and socially up to Shaughnessy Heights.

Another factor that contributed to the decline of the West End as an abode for the wealthy was the appearance of streetcar lines. By the turn of the century streetcars ran along Pender, Robson, Davie, and Denman Streets, making the area easily accessible to those who could not afford their own transportation. Also, commercial development followed the tracks, creeping down Robson and Davie and ultimately along Denman. The fact that Vancouver didn't begin to put zoning laws in place until 1927 meant that just about anything could be built. Soon apartment blocks began to appear, and by 1910 there were over 400 suites for rent west of Burrard Street. By the 1920s, the larger homes began to be converted into rooming houses or suites, and this trend continued until single-family residences became a rarity in the West End.

The West End's revitalization began in the mid-fifties, when high-rise apartments first made their appearance. While West End redevelopment has not been without problems, for many people this area has once again become a popular and attractive place to live.

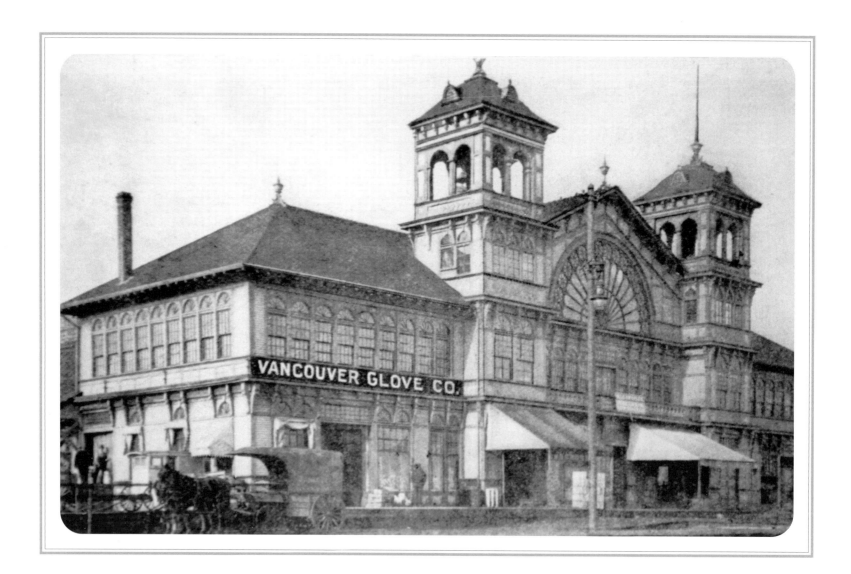

THE CITY MARKET

Vancouver's first market hall stood on the west side of Westminster Avenue, now Main Street, between Hastings and Pender. It was a substantial brick building that, after being remodelled in 1897, became the city hall. The decision of the city fathers to appropriate this building for their own use left Vancouver without a public market of any sort, and it left farmers from Lulu Island, Sea Island, and the Fraser Valley without a place where they could sell their produce directly to the public at reasonable prices.

Farmers believed that an ideal location for a public market would have its own wharf, making it possible for a small steamer to bring them and their produce from communities along the Fraser River. The idea of a public market was equally popular with city folk of the day, who had learned to appreciate the advantages of buying directly from the producer. While a site on Burrard Inlet between Westminster and Gore Avenues had wide community support and the endorsement of the Vancouver Board of Trade, city council chose to ignore it. The new City Market was built on cheaper land on the west side of Westminster Avenue, immediately south of False Creek, which was at that time spanned by a bascule bridge. In those days, the east end of False Creek had not yet been filled in and extended nearly to Clarke Drive.

The building was very much in the style of a Victorian exhibition hall. Designed by W.T. Whiteway, a Newfoundlander who had designed the World (Sun) Tower and a number of Vancouver schools, the structure was two storeys high and 130 by 150 feet. The contract for its construction was awarded to Bayfield and Williams on November 5, 1907, for $25,233.

The opening of the new City Market on August 15, 1908, was a grand success, attracting 3,000 people. A hindquarter of mutton was the prize awarded to the market's first customer, a Mrs. Allen of Columbia Street. The auction of horses and cattle on the market wharf also attracted a large crowd. It wasn't long, though, before success turned to failure. The location was such that a visit to the market involved a special trip. There were no stores or retail businesses anywhere near its site, which, today, is occupied by the Citygate development.

By the early 1920s the building was no longer used as a market. It was, instead, rented by the city to a number of small businesses – outfits like the Cement Laundry Tray Company, Wall's Fish and Fish Ball Company, Shellshear's Poultry, and Pearson Wire and Iron Works. An inauspicious end came early on the morning of November 10, 1925, when the building was completely destroyed by fire. All that firefighters and police could rescue were some of Mr. Shellshear's chickens.

One wonders how Whiteway's fanciful market hall might have fared had it been built on Burrard Inlet, where most people wanted it. The remote site chosen on the south side of False Creek, by the penny-wise-and-pound-foolish men of city council, doomed it to failure from the beginning.

New Westminster – "The Proper Place For Lunatics"

In 1871, it was reported in the BC Legislature "that the Dominion Government had declined to take charge of the lunatics of BC as it might be too large an undertaking." This left the responsibility squarely on provincial shoulders. Partly to appease the people of New Westminster, who had expected their city to become the provincial capital, it was decided that the "Lunatic Asylum" would be built in the Royal City. Until that time, the mentally ill would continue to be housed in the jails of Victoria and New Westminster.

Plans were drawn up in Victoria, and in 1876 a Victoria contractor began to build the new asylum. In an appropriate act of lunacy it was built to accommodate twenty-four patients, even though there were already thirty-five housed in temporary quarters in Victoria. The 125-by-25-foot brick building was two storeys high. Much to their annoyance, it was built on the cricket pitch the people of New Westminster had cleared years before. They watched in dismay as a chain gang from the neighbouring jail began constructing the asylum.

On May 17, 1878, twelve male and four female patients, accompanied by three male keepers and a matron, arrived from Victoria on the *Enterprise*. In the legislature, the member for Comox, Dr. John Ash, obviously a man of limited compassion, expressed concern that the asylum might be made too comfortable, tempting people to flock in, while Robert Smith of Yale said he had always felt New Westminster was "the proper place for lunatics." Within a year, forty-one patients were occupying a building designed for twenty-four. Despite Dr. Ash's concerns, in July 1884 a contract was let to build a north wing, which would increase capacity to seventy, and to make general improvements to a building that was more like a prison than a hospital.

The list of "disorders" suffered by the eight new patients admitted in 1884 included: nervous trouble, masturbation, injury to the head, intemperance, fright, and one unknown. It was an era in which mental illness was little understood, and the number of patients continued to grow – by 1897 there were already 203 – with the result that additions to the asylum were being built every few years. With expansion, staffing slowly improved. By 1890 the asylum had a full-time resident doctor, and in 1893 the first trained psychiatric nurse was added to the staff. By 1900, it was being recommended that retarded patients not be housed with mentally ill patients; it was also recognized that patients had to have constructive ways of occupying their time.

In July 1905, eighteen patients started clearing land for what became Colony Farm in 1911, and on April 1, 1913, Essondale, a new mental hospital, opened in Coquitlam. During the 1920s there was a gradual transfer of patients – the mentally ill being moved to the new hospital, leaving the "feeble-minded" in the old building in New Westminster. On April 1, 1950, the old asylum became The Woodland School in recognition of its educational function. Woodlands is currently being phased out. An 1899 recommendation of the asylum's resident physician that retarded patients should be kept in their own homes and communities is at last being fully acted upon, almost a century too late for some.

THE *EMPRESS OF INDIA*

While service had been inaugurated in 1887 through the use of chartered ships, it was not until an Imperial mail contract was signed by the British government on July 15, 1889, that the CPR placed an order for three trans-Pacific liners of its own. The vessels were built at Barrow in Furness, England, cost $1,200,000 each. The ships, large for their time at 5,906 gross tonnes, were equipped with triple expansion engines and twin screws but were not particularly innovative in design. In fact they were among the last steamships built that were equipped to carry sails. The ships were to be "empresses," and the *Empress of India,* the first of the trio, was launched on August 30, 1890. Together with its sister ships, the *Empress of China* and the *Empress of Japan,* it was the epitome of luxury, with stained glass, the finest hardwoods, silk upholstery, and rich carpets. Its staterooms even had both heat and electric light. The CPR spared little expense in order to be sure that its ships would be the finest on the Pacific.

The *Empress of India* arrived on the BC coast on April 28, 1891, having travelled by way of Suez, India, and the Orient, providing a luxury cruise for those who made the positioning run from Liverpool to Vancouver. The initial North Pacific crossing was made in 11 days, 7 hours, and 27 minutes, establishing a new speed record. The ship was designed to carry 160 saloon or first-class passengers, 40 second-class passengers and as many as 700 passengers in steerage. The steerage space was dual purpose: it could be used either for passengers, or for cargo.

While the three *Empresses* were fast – they had to average 16 knots to keep the mail contract – in high seas they could roll in a way that was uncomfortable for all passengers, regardless of whether they were travelling saloon class or steerage. It is hard to imagine what it must have been like to be one of 700 steerage passengers cooped up for upwards of eleven days, crossing the North Pacific in a ship that rolled twenty degrees even in seas that were only moderately rough!

The *Empress of India* served with majesty for twenty-five years. When it left for the Orient on August 22, 1914, even though war had been declared ten days earlier, few realized this would be the last time the *Empress of India* would be seen in Vancouver. On reaching Hong Kong the ship was ordered to Bombay, where the captain learned it was to be fitted out as a hospital ship. The vessel had been sold to the Maharajah of Gwalior for £85,000, and he, as a patriotic gesture, proposed to equip and maintain it as his personal contribution to the war effort. The *Empress of India* was appropriately renamed *Loyalty.* During the war, it made forty-one voyages, carrying 15,406 patients. After the First World War, the *Loyalty* had a short, unsuccessful career as a passenger vessel under Indian ownership. It was laid up in March 1921 and sold for scrap in 1923. One wonders if, somewhere in a back corner of a scrapyard in India, there is a rather elderly looking figurehead of Queen Victoria waiting to be brought home to Vancouver.

THE ST. ALICE HOTEL BUS

Pictured is the St. Alice Hotel's bus – a Rapid – on its way to Harrison Hot Springs. It has just met the train at Agassiz and is bringing a new contingent of guests to the hotel. To most, the name "St. Alice Hotel" will be unfamiliar. In the 1990s the major hotel at Harrison Hot Springs advertises itself as "the Harrison." But *that* hotel wasn't built until 1926, some six years after its predecessor, the St. Alice, had burned down. Perhaps we should go back to the beginning of the story.

It was in 1846 that Harrison Lake was first explored by a European, Alexander Anderson of the Hudson's Bay Company. The lake became important to the colonial government in 1858, when Governor Douglas ordered a road built from the top of the lake to Lillooet and on to the Cariboo gold fields. The First Nations people, of course, had known for centuries that there were thermal springs at both the lower end of Harrison Lake and on the Lillooet River beyond the upper end of the lake. While no one knows what White person first discovered the springs, we do know that Judge Mathew Baillie Begbie named them when he passed through the area in 1859. He called the hot springs on the Lillooet River "St. Agnes' Well" and those at the lower end of Harrison Lake "St. Alice's Well." Agnes and Alice were the daughters of Sir James Douglas.

J.R. Brown was the original owner of the St. Alice Hotel, a three-storey frame structure with wide verandas. It had opened on November 1, 1886, and could accommodate 130 guests. As well, an annex was built adjacent to the hot springs to accommodate guests too weak to walk the short distance from the hotel. While the Harrison has largely traded on its appeal as an upscale resort facility, the St. Alice was promoted primarily as a health spa or sanatorium, featuring the therapeutic properties of the potash and sulphur baths.

When the hotel opened there was still no road into the hot springs. In that first year, guests made their way up the Harrison River by boat. In 1887, however, the five-mile road between Agassiz and Harrison Hot Springs was completed. The "road," built at a cost of $3,050, was an eight-foot-wide pathway cleared through trees and bush, with a ditch on either side. While our picture dates from around 1910, the road still seems to be less than the "fine carriage road" promotional materials of the period claimed it to be.

The St. Alice Hotel's first bus was a Studebaker Electric, beautifully finished with fine leather upholstery and shining brass trim. Although quiet, it wasn't very practical, as its thousand-pound battery had to be recharged after every trip. Recharging took so much time that the bus could only make one round trip a day to Agassiz! It wasn't too long before it was replaced by a noisy, but much more efficient, Rapid – a chain-driven vehicle powered by a two-cylinder internal combustion engine.

Fire!

No celebration in Vancouver's early days was complete without fire engines being part of the passing parade. While the cause of the celebration pictured remains a mystery, girls in white frocks and boys in shirtsleeves suggest summertime, and summertime suggests Dominion Day. Before the First World War, a parade was a *must* on July first.

The crowd of admirers are watching the Vancouver Fire Department's horse-drawn, seventy-five-foot aerial ladder pass along Hastings Street at Richards. The aerial ladder was built in 1899 by the Waterous Engine Works Company of Brantford, Ontario, at a cost of $3,400. Put into service on October 21, 1899, it was in regular use until 1916. Vancouver, having burned to the ground on June 13, 1886, was never penny-pinching when it came to its fire department.

Vancouver's first fire chief was certainly the right man, at the right time, in the right job. John Howe Carlisle was chief from 1886 until 1928. He was far in advance of most men in his profession. In 1890 he persuaded city council to install Gamewell electric fire-alarm boxes, thus making Vancouver the first city in North America to have automatic call boxes on its streets.

The city first bought gasoline-powered vehicles in 1907. They were the first three motorized fire engines built by the Seagrave Company of Columbus Ohio. On March 1, 1908, Chief Carlisle opened the first Vancouver fire hall to be built specifically for the new fire-fighting equipment. This was Fire Hall Number Six, at Nicola and Nelson Streets, in the West End. Not to be left behind, either literally or figuratively, the fire chief also took delivery of a two-cylinder McLaughlin-Buick touring car. As far as he was concerned, the day of the horse and buggy was over, and in his annual report for 1907, Chief Carlisle recommended that all future equipment be self-propelled. Vancouver was not only the first city in Canada to purchase motorized fire-fighting equipment, but, in 1917, it became home to Canada's first completely motorized fire department.

Chief Carlisle, the firefighters, and the people of Vancouver had much of which to be proud. In 1909, the Vancouver Fire Department was judged to be third best in the world. A committee of international experts concluded that only London, England, and Leipzig, Saxony, were superior to Vancouver in terms of fire-fighting equipment and efficiency.

Amazingly, given the size of Vancouver, the number of major fires has been very small. Part of the reason is that, beginning way back in 1911, Carlisle hired two fire wardens, who were, as he reported "employed inspecting buildings in the city, and, maintained on motor-cycles, were constantly patrolling the business and factory districts." The use of motor-cycles in 1911 not only says something about Chief Carlisle's vision and imagination, it also says a lot about his ability to have his way with city councils of his day.

Vancouver General Hospital

The first hospital in what is now Vancouver was a nine-bed cottage hospital belonging to the CPR. It stood at the side of the track between Hawks and Heatly Streets. Opened in 1886, it was brought into existence to care for workers injured on the job while extending the railway's main line from Port Moody to Vancouver. In 1887 the city took responsibility for the small hospital, henceforth to be known as City Hospital.

As Vancouver was a port city, there was always a high level of concern for health and sanitation. In 1887, Dr. J.M. Lefevre, the CPR's surgeon and an alderman, convinced city council to appoint a medical health officer. In the same year, the city's health by-law provided free medical and nursing care for the poor, either at home or in City Hospital.

A new City Hospital opened on September 25, 1888. Located on Pender Street, between Cambie and Beatty, it was a frame building on a stone foundation. The new hospital had thirty-five beds and was under the control of the city's Health Committee. Brick additions, which were completed in 1902, brought City Hospital's capacity to fifty patients. Some other important things happened in 1902. First of all, City Hospital was incorporated by a provincial act as Vancouver General Hospital. Through incorporation it became a private, non-profit institution managed by its own board, which was elected by a general membership. Equally significant, in the same year two city blocks, comprising five and a half acres, were purchased in Fairview for a new hospital.

Voters approved a money by-law in 1903 that funded construction of the first building on the Fairview site. Grant and Henderson were the architects, and they designed the building pictured. Located on the corner of Tenth Avenue and Heather Street, the new hospital, built of stone and pressed brick, featured three floors plus basement. Its many open balconies reflected the importance attached to fresh air as an aid to healing and health. The skylighted operating rooms on the top floor of the east wing suggest that electric light was still considered neither ideal nor reliable, although the new hospital did have its own generating plant.

When the new Vancouver General Hospital opened in January of 1906, forty-seven patients were transferred from the old downtown building to the new Fairview facility. The new building was initially intended to accommodate 104 patients. It seems that expanding facilities to keep up with growing need has been a Vancouver General Hospital fact of life from day one!

Still to be found hidden away in the immense complex that is now Vancouver Hospital and Health Sciences Centre is a part of the original building, which opened in 1906. It is called the Heather Pavilion. Some things, it appears, were meant to last.

GRANVILLE STREET

One of the advantages that accrued to officials in the colonial service, and to their friends, was that of being "in the know" regarding where and when to invest in land. The shores of Burrard Inlet were made particularly attractive for speculation by the existence of the Moodyville Mill on the North Shore and by Stamp's Hastings Mill on the south side of the inlet. It seemed like everyone from Attorney-General H.P.P. Crease to Colonel Moody's former secretary, Robert Burnaby, owned district lots of 160 acres on Burrard Inlet, False Creek, or English Bay.

By 1885, CPR officials decided that the rail line would not end at Port Moody but twelve miles farther west at Coal Harbour's deep-water moorage. All who held land grants or owned real estate in the Granville townsite were more than pleased when the provincial government gave the railway a subsidy of 480 acres on Coal Harbour and 5,795 acres south of False Creek as an "incentive" to do what it had already determined to do anyway. The government's 480-acre grant included 8 acres in the form of 39 specific lots within Granville townsite. As well, landowners like John Robson (who was later to become premier), the Oppenheimer brothers, Dr. Israel Powell, and the "Three Greenhorns" all donated land to the CPR. The Greenhorns – John Morton, Samuel Brighouse, and William Hailstone – got their nickname because, in 1862, they went prospecting in an out-of-the-way place that experienced prospectors considered to have no potential whatsoever. The place was Coal Harbour. The Greenhorns, who, for twenty-five years held on to their 550-acre pre-emption in what was to become the West End, donated a third of their property to the railway. Why all this unnecessary munificence? It was a way of guaranteeing larger future gains: the railway would be actively promoting the sale of its lands, and the neighbouring properties were sure to be of high value.

Vancouver streets were laid out in 1885 and 1886 by Lauchlan Hamilton, the CPR's land commissioner, with the assistance of H. Cambie and H. Abbott. It was not by accident that the CPR's station and wharf were both at the foot of Granville Street, with the company's office, the Hotel Vancouver, and the opera house being located farther south. The move was intended to pull the centre of the city westward, and it did so most successfully. It wasn't long before the Bank of Montreal, the Bank of Commerce, the Hudson's Bay Company's store, and other enterprising businesses relocated along Granville Street.

Pictured (ca. 1903 or 1904) is the east side of Granville, north of the Hudson's Bay Company's store, looking towards Dunsmuir. The little wooden building with the tipsy awning housed Martin Daiber's Delta Meat Market. This 1886 wooden building, with its wild-west false front, was one of the last remaining frame buildings in the downtown area. An 1887 by-law required all buildings in the downtown area to be built of "fire-proof" materials. Beyond the butcher shop was Joseph Turner's Liquor Store and the New York Block, which housed the CPR's ticket, telegraph, and land offices until the turn of the century. Other buildings along the block provided retail space for a tobacconist, tea merchant, milliner, lace shop merchant, shoe merchant, and druggist: all operators of businesses that would front on the "high street" in any Edwardian town of consequence.

HOTEL ELYSIUM

ealtors tell us that the first three things to consider when buying a property are location, location, and location! Marriott and Fellows, local realtors, certainly ignored the wisdom of their profession when they decided to build the Elysium Hotel on West Pender between Thurlow and Bute. The ill-conceived product of a building boom, the 100-room hotel opened on April 1, 1911. It was designed by E.Y. Grassett and Sholto Smith in a nondescript style that was probably intended to have a residential feel about it. A marginal operation at best, in 1917 the Elysium became the Returned Soldiers' Club. By 1920 it was again a commercial hotel.

One interesting chapter in the Elysium's story concerns a 1938 beer licence application. Not surprisingly the application was opposed by the BC Hotel Association, which represented Vancouver's sixty-three tavern owners. At first, city council agreed there should be no more licences, then it was realized that the Canadian National Railways' new hotel on Georgia would be opening in 1939 and would be wanting a licence. The city fathers hit upon a convenient solution to the problem, saying no further licences would be recommended for hotels half a block below Georgia!

To help relieve the city's wartime housing shortage, the Elysium was turned into forty-six family suites under the federal government's Home Conversion Plan. After spending its final years as the Park Plaza Hotel, the building was torn down in the 1970s and was replaced by an office tower at 1130 West Pender Street.

HOTEL EUROPE

The Hotel Europe in Gastown is a Vancouver landmark. It was built by Angelo Colari in 1909 on the site where he had started business in 1886. Within easy walking distance of coastal steamship docks, the Europe was well located to meet the needs of loggers and fishers as well as commercial travellers, who regularly made their way up and down the Coast.

The Europe was designed by Parr and Fee, successful commercial architects of their day. The original design called for a building of eight storeys, with a series of nine oriel windows on each floor extending from the second to the eighth floor. A revised building only reached six storeys, and the series of rather fussy bay windows was replaced by attractive flat sides of brick veneer, which covered reinforced concrete. The structure was capped by a simple yet impressive cornice. The Europe was the first major building made of reinforced concrete in the city and was advertised as the first fire-proof building in Western Canada.

When the Europe opened, its ground floor was divided between the entrance hall, dining room, and bar. The basement, which extends under the sidewalks and is lighted by pavement prisms, was fitted out as a spacious hall that could be reached through a separate entrance at the west end of the building by a broad marble staircase. A further part of the basement, lighted by heavy glass blocks set into the sidewalks above, was intended for public baths (which, as it happened, were never installed). Today the Hotel Europe is preserved as a heritage building and provides much-needed comfortable and attractive social housing in Gastown.

THE FIRST HOTEL VANCOUVER

On December 31, 1881, William Van Horne became general manager of the CPR, and, as was his wont, he soon seemed to be generally managing everything. In only a few years, he would complete the railway from Montreal to Port Moody, then extend it twelve miles to Granville, a village he would be instrumental in renaming "Vancouver." He would establish a steamship line to sail to the Orient, financially assisted by a $60,000 annual Imperial mail subsidy coaxed out of the British government. And in February 1886, he would recommend to his directors that a hotel be built in Vancouver. The proposed Hotel Vancouver was the first in what would become a corporate chain of luxury hotels.

Thomas Sorby, an architect with offices in both Vancouver and Victoria, was commissioned to design the hotel. He worked quickly, and construction began on July 22, 1886. The CPR chose the southwest corner of Granville and Georgia for its hotel, a site opposed by city council because it was thought not to be central enough. The Hotel Vancouver opened May 16, just in time for the arrival of the first transcontinental train on May 23, 1887.

Although the building was budgeted at half a million dollars, Sorby constructed what he called "a building without architecture." The railway had done some economizing, and what was to have been a structure built "in simplified chateau style" ended up being described in the local press as "an exceedingly ugly workhouse." In 1894 an imposing brick and stone addition was built along the Granville Street frontage, south of Sorby's building. The effect was described by local wags as "reminding one of a farmer who has married an aristocratic wife."

By 1900 the Hotel Vancouver was again too small, and the CPR announced that it intended to demolish Sorby's building and replace it with a larger hotel. Francis Rattenbury, who had designed the new Parliament Buildings in Victoria, was awarded the commission in 1901. He designed a building in the Chateau style and planned to erect the hotel in stages so that it could remain open during construction. By the time he began building a wing of eighty rooms facing onto Georgia and Howe Streets, the original design had altered dramatically.

Construction began December 17, 1901, not in the style of a French chateau but, rather, in the style of an Italian Renaissance palazzo. It seemed that railway management had decided to reserve the Chateau style for resorts, favouring the Renaissance style for its urban hotels. As it turned out, the west wing, which was completed in 1905, was all that was ever built of Rattenbury's hotel. For some reason that has never been clear, the CPR decided not to proceed with the project. Thus it was that Sorby's "economized" chateau and Rattenbury's palazzo stood in rather unhappy juxtaposition until the second Hotel Vancouver was built on the same site a decade later.

HASTINGS STREET

Vancouver's Hastings Street looks hot, dry, and dusty in this 1905 photograph. The pace could only be described as summer-day leisurely: wagons meander, pedestrians saunter, and even the streetcar seems to be going nowhere in a hurry. Indeed, were it travelling at any speed the wagon crossing the track in front of it would be in serious trouble! The picture focuses on the 300-block West Hastings, looking from Hamilton Street towards Homer Street. In 1905 this block was very much at the centre of the city, providing the right address for both merchants and professional people. The building in the left foreground was the Inns of Court Building. Being right across the street from the court house, which stood on Government Square (now Victory Square), it provided a prestigious location for some of the city's leading legal firms. The Bank of Hamilton, named after the Ontario town where it was founded, occupied the ground floor. It was one of the twenty chartered banks doing business in the city before the First World War.

The fact that the Bank of Hamilton was on Hamilton Street was pure coincidence. The street was named after Lauchlan Hamilton, the CPR's first land commissioner. Before he came to Vancouver, he had surveyed and laid out the streets of Regina, Moose Jaw, Swift Current, and Calgary. In 1883 he was instructed by William Van Horne, the CPR's general manager, to survey the company's land grant in what is now downtown Vancouver. He was not only to lay out the streets, but also to name them.

The actual survey took place in the fall of 1885, and the first stake was driven into the earth at what is now the southwest corner of Hastings and Hamilton. The site is marked by a plaque, which reads: "Here stood Hamilton, first Land Commissioner, Canadian Pacific Railway, 1885. In the silent solitude of the primeval forest Hamilton drove a wooden stake in the earth and commenced to measure an empty land into the streets of Vancouver." The florid language of a bygone day successfully hides the fact that the marker wasn't erected until 1952! The first four streets he named were: Hastings, which led through the woods to the old townsite of the same name; Abbott and Cambie, which honoured two of his fellow CPR regional officials; and, of course, Hamilton, which was named after himself. Interestingly, the 300-block West Hastings was also home to two early private business colleges, the Pacific Business College and the Sprott-Shaw Business Institute.

The roadbed itself, as was that of a number of Vancouver streets, was made of cedar blocks set on end. While their chief disadvantage was that these end-grain cedar blocks could be extremely slippery when wet, they had yet another one: they burned too well. To celebrate Lord Roberts's Relief of Mafeking in South Africa on May 17, 1900, local citizens set a great bonfire in the middle of Hastings Street between Hamilton and Cambie. The fire burned brilliantly, as did the city's new wood-block pavement. A great hole had to be filled in and the burned blocks replaced. If one knows where to look, one may still find a few Vancouver streets in Fairview between Main and Cambie where the old cedar paving blocks lurk beneath the asphalt.

"Nor Any Drop To Drink"

"Water, water, every where / Nor any drop to drink." One might be forgiven for thinking of Coleridge's *Rime of the Ancient Mariner* in connection with early Vancouver. It seems that William Van Horne, who generally thought of everything, forgot all about a water supply when he chose the south side of Burrard Inlet as the western terminus of the CPR. The citizens had no readily accessible source worth talking about: Mount Pleasant's Tea Swamp and Trout Lake (farther east) were about it. Vancouver's pioneer settlers either dug wells, collected rain water in cisterns, or bought water that had been shipped by barge from the North Shore.

Enter George Alexander Keefer, the engineer who was responsible for surveying the CPR's route through the Rockies and Fraser Canyon. He was living in Victoria, where, together with some wealthy friends, he saw the potential for making money by solving Vancouver's water supply problem. On April 6, 1886, their Vancouver Water Works Company received its charter from the provincial legislature. Keefer had the advantage of having as his uncle Thomas Coltrin Keefer, who was probably the greatest hydraulic engineer of his day. Uncle Thomas, who lived in Ottawa, provided invaluable help and advice.

A dam site was chosen six and a half miles up the Capilano River. On April 18, 1888, a 384-foot rock-filled wooden crib dam was completed. It was 388 feet above sea level, which meant that a simple gravity system could carry water successfully to the city. Plans called for two pipes to be laid under the First Narrows in case one was ever damaged. On August 18, 1888, the first line of 1,104 feet of one-foot diameter flexible joint pipe was laid. Water from the Capilano River first ran through the new system on March 26, 1889.

But what has all this to do with a summer's day in Stanley Park? Well, the picture is of Pipe Line (now Pipeline) Road, which runs along the east side of the rose garden to a point on Burrard Inlet west of Lumberman's Arch. After crossing the First Narrows, the city's first water main passed along under this road. It then went under Coal Harbour, up Georgia Street to Granville, down Granville to Hastings, and along Hastings to Westminster Avenue. On June 11, 1890, the second main was laid under the First Narrows. Westminster Avenue was renamed Main Street in 1911 because the latter name conjured up visions of big, go-getting cities.

Keefer's Vancouver Water Works Company spent $300,000 and twenty-two months on the project. There were many false starts, difficulties, and setbacks, but the system worked. In fact it worked so well that in 1889 the city's Fire, Water and Light Committee recommended that the assets of the company be purchased outright. As it happened, the water company's charter allowed the city to buy it out after giving twelve months' written notice. On September 15, 1891, the city's voters authorized the purchase of the Vancouver Water Works Company for $448,922.12. Vancouver got its water system, Keefer deservedly got a street named after him, and Stanley Park got Pipeline Road!

ENGLISH BAY, 1904

This 1904 picture of English Bay shows the beach in its last year of unregulated development. The next year, English Bay, or First Beach as it was sometimes called, came under Parks Board control and regulation. Even though it was just a few hundred feet of cleared shoreline, it was highly popular, attracting large crowds in summer. The vast expanse of sand seen today represents the investment of a lot of work and money: English Bay's natural state was rocks, mud, and barnacles. Regarding its popularity, it has to be remembered that much of present-day downtown Vancouver was still residential in 1904, and English Bay would have been considered within easy walking distance. As well, in 1904, beyond the cleared beach area to the east were camps – tent colonies set up by city residents for the summer – and nondescript shacks that were home to squatters. West of Gilford Street and extending as far as Stanley Park were some handsome cottages. They were owned and occupied for the season by a number of affluent citizens who chose not to live year round in the West End.

Returning to our picture, it illustrates the uncontrolled development of the day. On the far left are two privately owned bathhouses: the Pavilion and the Crescent. They provided changing rooms on their lower floors and places for light refreshment on their upper floors. Behind the two bathhouses is the English Bay Club, a "men-only" social club. Next is the public path to the beach and then Simpson's Boat House, where rowboats could be rented.

The long white building is the city-owned bathhouse, topped by a bandstand. When not being used for concerts, the bandstand could be rented for private parties. On the right of the picture, in front of the public and communal bathhouse, are six little private dressing rooms for the more modest bathers. Beyond the right-hand end of the picture stood a popular water slide, and beyond that, at the foot of Burnaby Street, stood a huge white boulder. This large rock marked a dividing line: ladies bathed to the west of it, gentlemen to the east. Joe Fortes, English Bay's beloved lifeguard, saw to it that no young blades ventured beyond the boulder into what was literally no man's land!

Improvements came rapidly to English Bay after it came under Parks Board jurisdiction. In 1905 a new $6,000 wooden bathing pavilion was built, and in 1906 water safety equipment was provided for the first time. The pleasure pier was built between Chilco and Gilford Streets in 1907, and in 1909 the first concrete bathhouse was built. In its final years this building served as the city's first aquarium. In 1911 the Parks Board set out to buy up all waterfront property along Beach Avenue. The final piece of land wasn't acquired until the 1980s. Looking at English Bay and Beach Avenue today, Vancouver's citizens can appreciate not only Parks Board policy, but also the patience and persistence that has opened up the waterfront for all to enjoy.

To London, To London, To See The King

Pictured at the North Vancouver ferry wharf are three First Nations chiefs about to leave for London to put Native grievances before King Edward VII. Our picture was taken on July 3, 1906. The man at the centre of the photo, with the robe over his arm, is Chief Joe Capilano. Travelling to Buckingham Palace with him were Chief Charlie Tsipeymutt of Cowichan on Vancouver Island and Chief Bazel David of Bonaparte in the Interior.

Until after the Second World War, aboriginal peoples were wards of the Crown; in the eyes of the law they were "as infants." In British Columbia they could not pre-empt land, vote, or buy liquor unless they forswore their tribal allegiance and severed all tribal relations. While tribes, through their chiefs and councillors, could enact by-laws for the regulation of minor affairs on the reserves, such enactments required government approval before they could be enforced.

One of the concerns the chiefs wanted to share with the King related to what we today call land claims. Even before the First World War, Native leaders were arguing that, except in a few instances, their title to Crown lands had never been relinquished. The provincial government of the day not only refused to recognize any such title, it would not even allow the question to be placed before the Imperial Privy Council. The government argued that, in setting up reserves, it had adequately dealt with the Native population. And because they were wards of the Crown, the three chiefs felt that they had a special relationship with the king and that he would give them a sympathetic hearing and because of their understanding of the power of hereditary chiefs, they had an exaggerated belief in the power of the monarch and what he could do for them.

The chiefs were graciously received by King Edward, who was a man of great personal charm. More important, he, like his mother, Queen Victoria, probably had a more genuine concern for the indigenous peoples of his Empire than did most of his colonial ministers, administrators, and civil servants. While the visit to London accomplished little politically, Chief Capilano always remembered it as one of the great moments of his life. He treasured the gift the king had given him, "as one chief to another."

The way to the States
from Mission Jct. B.C.

A One-Horsepower Bridge

In 1883 the promoters of the Bellingham Bay and British Columbia Railway asked the CPR to connect with their proposed line at Huntingdon/Sumas on the international boundary. The CPR declined this invitation but had a change of heart in 1889, when it was apparent that the Great Northern Railway would soon complete its line to the south side of the Fraser River at New Westminster. The CPR began construction of its connecting line from Mission to Huntington in February, 1891. Before the branch line could be completed, however, a bridge had to be built over the Fraser.

Work began on the original wooden bridge in 1889. In addition to the trestles at either end, it consisted of eight fixed Howe trusses and a Howe truss swing span. When built it was the only bridge over the Fraser below Lytton, and it was reputed to be the world's longest wooden bridge. The silver "last spike" was driven at Sumas by the governor of Washington on June 22, 1891, and the railway was open for business. The swing span was opened and closed by horsepower, and the horse's name was "Charlie." The animal was harnessed to the mechanism in the centre of the span and walked around in circles, opening or closing the bridge as required. Charlie was stabled in a shed attached to the side of the swing span in winter and in a field on the south bank of the river in summer. Whenever a sternwheeler whistled, Charlie went to work.

Over the years the bridge's wooden piers were replaced by concrete ones, and its timber trusses gave way to steel beams. In 1903 the 233-foot swing span was replaced by a steel span. The rebuilding of the rest of the bridge took place between 1908 and 1910. It was also at this time that Charlie was replaced by a gasoline engine.

The Canadian Bridge Construction Company was responsible for the rebuilding of the bridge. On March 17, 1910, the local paper mentioned that "most of the men have been very popular ... and many regret to see their departure, especially some of the fairer sex with whom the young men made themselves acquainted." We are also told that the Methodist Church had a party for the construction workers, at which "sixty-five guests attended and did justice to the good things provided."

In 1927 the bridge deck was planked for vehicular traffic. Even though it was only wide enough for one-way traffic, it was a welcome improvement over the old ferry service. The bridge continued to provide a crossing for both trains and automobiles until 1973, when a highway bridge was opened. Although railway passenger service to Huntingdon and Sumas was discontinued on June 30, 1959, the old Mission Bridge continues to carry freight traffic to and from the United States.

The photo, looking through the bridge to the south side of the Fraser, dates from 1910 or 1911. Whoever took the photograph not only managed to provide us with a picture of the bridge newly rebuilt, but also with an impressive and clever study in perspective.

ST. ANN'S SCHOOL FOR YOUNG LADIES

On June 20, 1865, two sisters of the Roman Catholic Order of St. Ann arrived in New Westminster. They had come from Victoria at the invitation of Bishop L.J. D'Herbomez, OMI, to open a school. The Order of St. Ann was a teaching order, and its mother house was located in Quebec. Before the arrival of the sisters the bishop had already purchased an acre and a half of land with a 163-foot frontage on Albert Crescent. On it he had built the frame building that became St. Ann's Academy's first home.

The sisters placed an announcement in the *British Columbian* on July 13, stating they were "here and ready to receive pupils" for the first classes in September. They had wisely arrived at the beginning of the summer, both to allow time to recruit pupils and to give the citizens of the Royal City time to become accustomed to their presence. The Roman Catholic population was quite small, and nuns would not have been immediately welcomed by everyone in the community.

St. Ann's School for Young Ladies opened on September 5, 1865. There were five boarders and three day girls enrolled, the latter being the daughters of Captain William Irving. The school fees were forty-eight dollars per quarter, to be paid in advance, and there was an additional charge for music and painting. The school prospered, and within a decade it became obvious that a new and larger building was needed.

The cornerstone for the seventy-three-by-thirty-nine-foot stone and brick building pictured was laid on August 15, 1877. Three storeys high, with a circular tower and a mansard roof, the school was a most attractive building. Its site gave it a commanding view up and down the Fraser River. It was officially opened on April 17, 1878. Not ready in time for the opening, the chiming clock in the tower was dedicated separately on October 27, 1878.

The school was a great success, and in 1912 a wing was added to the east end of the building. The addition meant that fifty boarders and 200 day pupils could be accommodated. Although St. Ann's escaped New Westminster's great fire of 1898, it was severely damaged in 1944, when a fire started by a student gutted the two top floors of the building. It was rebuilt minus the mansard roof and with a much simplified tower.

In 1954, when St. Peter's Parochial School was built, the academy became a regional high school for girls. Times and needs were changing rapidly, and, in 1968, the sisters decided the time had come to close the school and sell the land. In the winter of 1968-69, the building was torn down. St. Ann's School for Young Ladies became one more completed chapter in New Westminster's book of memories.

THE CASTLE ON BEATTY STREET

After almost a century, the Beatty Street Drill Hall may look like a castle small children would create with their building blocks. Not so. Designed by the architects of the Department of Public Works in Ottawa, it was built to serve as the headquarters for the British Columbia regiment, the Duke of Connaught's Own Rifles.

Construction began in late 1899. The building has a frontage of 149 feet and is about as solid as a building can be. Its rafters are of iron, the drill hall floor is of wood blocks over concrete, and the armoury floor is of heavy wood. All this rests on a foundation of seven-by-four-foot granite blocks. The walls are all three and a half feet thick. Below street level, space was provided for a shooting gallery and a bowling alley.

The drill hall was opened with great fanfare on September 30, 1901, by no less a person than HRH the Duke of Cornwall and York, who, in 1910, would become King George V. The duke presented South African War medals to one nursing sister, one officer, and twenty-six other members of the regiment. The sister was Mary Affleck, who had gone overseas with the first contingent to sail from Canada at the outbreak of the Boer War. Reports of the day tell us that when Miss Affleck received her medal, she also received, according to the *Vancouver Daily Province*, "a sympathetic smile from the Duchess, who always appeared particularly pleased at the recognition of merit in members of her own sex." The Duchess is best remembered today as Queen Mary, the present queen's grandmother.

In our picture, members of the Duke of Connaught's Own Rifles are parading on what used to be called the Cambie Street Grounds – the block bordered by Beatty, Georgia, Dunsmuir, and Cambie Streets. In 1902, city voters had approved the expenditure for the purchase of four park sites from the CPR, and the Cambie Street Grounds proved the most popular. The grounds were convenient to the drill hall; to the Vancouver Athletic Club, with its headquarters on Dunsmuir; and to the city's high school, which was only a block away. Perhaps the most important reason for their popularity was the presence of Al Larwill.

Larwill had come to Vancouver in 1887 and lived on the edge of the grounds in a shack filled with sports equipment, which he loaned out. He was as devoted to kids as he was to sports, and he gave countless hours to organizing and coaching boys' lacrosse, cricket, baseball, and football (or soccer as it's now called). He died in 1911. Rather belatedly, in 1943, the Parks Board renamed the athletic grounds Larwill Park in his honour. Larwill Park disappeared in 1946, when, as part of a complicated land swap, the property was leased to the BC Electric as a site for a new bus depot. The bus depot has since gone, and the land, now in private hands, is being used for a parking lot.

SECOND BEACH

Second Beach was so-named to distinguish it from First Beach, better known as English Bay. Second Beach was popular even in the late 1880s, when it was not much more than a small recess amid the rocks, kelp, and barnacles. Perhaps it was the honky-tonk atmosphere of English Bay, with its concessions and attractions, that made Second Beach, which had none of these things, so attractive to families.

The Parks Board was well aware of the special nature of Second Beach and worked to enhance its appeal. In 1904, it erected the first bathing shed for ladies. Two years later both First and Second Beaches were equipped with water safety equipment. The city's first playground equipment, six swings, was bought in 1907 for Second Beach.

The Parks Board, as a matter of policy, was determined to keep Second Beach as a family beach. This meant that there would be no charge for the use of dressing rooms or other amenities. In 1912 it was proudly reported that a new bathhouse for women and children had been built at a cost of $13,687 – no small sum at that time. Men still had to take to the woods, of course! In the same year, the Parks Board terminated bathhouse leases at both English Bay and Kitsilano Beach, providing and maintaining free facilities at all city beaches.

Our picture, which probably dates from 1913, shows the new and attractive bathhouse. It was described in the Parks Board's Annual Report for 1912 as being

> for the exclusive use of women and children. Designed in California Mission style with broad overhanging eaves, it is built in a substantial manner with granite foundations, hollow tile walls, and reinforced concrete floors, the exterior walls being roughcast. The dressing booths are of honed polished slate, and throughout the building wood trim and finish has as far as possible been eliminated, the idea being to use nothing in the finished construction that would suffer damp and to make the building throughout as damp-proof as possible. In the main centre and situated on the top floor are public conveniences for women only, as are also a small rest room and balcony overlooking the bathing beach.

In 1924, Ceperley Meadows, a children's playground adjacent to the beach, was opened. Made possible through a bequest, the playground enhanced the idea that Second Beach was to be a family place. Eight years later a new salt-water pool dramatically changed the appearance of Second Beach. While it was not the city's first ocean pool, it was immensely popular.

In spite of, or perhaps because of, all the changes that have taken place over the years, Second Beach has remained very much a family-oriented beach, with features to meet the recreational need of young and old alike. Now a brand new multi-use shoreline pool continues that legacy.

THE CPR'S SECOND STATION

Vancouver's first CPR train station was a simple, two-storey, twenty-by-forty-foot frame structure that would not have been out of place in any small town in Western Canada. It was built in 1886-87 as part of the terminal complex designed by Thomas Sorby, and it was intended to serve as a passenger facility only for the first three or four months. However, it remained in use until the turn of the century, when it was replaced by the second station, a building of striking style and quality that stood on Cordova Street, right at the foot of Granville.

This second station, costing over $200,000, had all the necessities and amenities one would expect to find in so imposing a structure. Designed by Montreal architect Edward Maxwell, the building was an early example of the CPR Chateau style. Its massive turrets, one round and one octagonal, made the station as eye-catching as any High Victorian structure could wish to be. It also featured an impressive forty-two-foot arched entranceway of rusticated Calgary limestone. The building was faced in special moisture-resistant brick brought from Victoria, and a slate roof capped with copper added the final note of elegance to an eminently successful building.

A unique feature for a Canadian railway station was the arrangement in the street-level rotunda: the ticket offices formed an island in the centre of the room. And, of course, there was a separate ladies' waiting room on the main floor. Down one floor, at track level, were reception and departure areas. The upper storeys were eventually occupied by the land department, purchasing and accounting offices, and by what we would now call executive offices.

Unfortunately, this second station was built at the wrong time and in the wrong place. Even though the foundations were completed in 1892, the railway did not authorize further work until 1897, when Tomkin and Company got on with the actual construction, which took two years. The CPR delayed building because it was believed that the planned station would be too big for Vancouver. The irony was that when the building was opened in 1899, it was already too small for the growing city.

On June 19, 1907, the CPR announced its intention to build yet another station, this one to cost over a million dollars. The third station's site was such that the second station had to be razed in order to make room for the new building. The second station had completely disappeared by August 1914, when the present station opened for business. If one wonders what Maxwell's station might have been like, a trip to New Westminster might provide some hints. He designed the 1889 CPR station that still stands in the Royal City, now housing a small police detachment and a popular restaurant.

NEW WESTMINSTER'S COLUMBIA STREET

Before the days of "regional plans," "town centres," "freeways," and "ALRT," travelling from Vancouver to New Westminster meant much more than going from one part of the Greater Vancouver Regional District to another; it meant taking a trip between cities. Even though Vancouver and New Westminster were, and still are, only twelve miles apart, they were very different places. New Westminster has a character, charm, and life of its own.

New Westminster owed its existence to gold and to an "invasion" of Americans. After gold was discovered along the Fraser River in 1856, news quickly spread abroad, and by 1858 James Douglas, Governor of the Colony of Vancouver Island, was concerned about hordes of California miners rushing north. He felt Britain must reaffirm its control of the mainland before it was too late. His concern was heard and shared in London, and the Crown Colony of British Columbia came into being on November 19, 1858. Douglas, while retaining the governorship of the neighbouring colony of Vancouver Island, became the new colony's first governor. As he worked to establish law and order on the mainland, he was supported by the presence of the Royal Engineers, under the command of Colonel Richard Moody.

One of Moody's first assignments was to assist Douglas in choosing a site, on navigable waters, for the colony's capital. Their efforts concentrated on the Fraser River, and although Douglas preferred Derby (Fort Langley), Moody recommended a site on high ground on the north side of the Fraser, which would be easier to defend should push come to shove with the Americans. Moody's logic prevailed, and Douglas accepted his recommendation. Since the bureaucrats in the new colony couldn't agree on what to call the new capital, Queen Victoria was invited to select a name. She chose "New Westminster."

Columbia Street remained New Westminster's principal retail street, from its days as a colonial capital until the advent of the shopping mall. Pictured in 1909, it had a quiet, summer's-day look about it. The streetcar on the single-track City and Sapperton line is waiting for passengers from the next Vancouver tram before embarking on its trip to Distillery Road (now Braid Street) in Sapperton, an old community on the eastern edge of New Westminster. The tracks crossing Columbia Street in the foreground lead into the interurban station.

The tranquility of the scene suggests this photo was taken mid-week at high noon rather on a Saturday, when Columbia Street was alive with both local shoppers and country folk from across the river. People would come to shop, sell, trade, and enjoy the highlight of their week – an afternoon or evening in town. Columbia Street didn't remain as it appears in our 1909 picture for long. By 1912 stylish new office buildings, stores, and banks, together with new paving and ornamental lighting, had given the street a more substantial, more urban, look.

A Small-Town Station

The station pictured was the second built by the CPR in Mission. The original station stood in front of St. Mary's Mission and Indian Residential School until 1891, when it was moved to the "Y" in the track. The "Y" came into being in the same year, when the CPR built a line from Mission across the Fraser River to Huntingdon on the international border. There, connection was made with American lines to Bellingham and Seattle. The station was again moved in 1904, this time to where the present station stands.

Mission was an important junction on the CPR line; both passenger and freight trains came and went all day long from Seattle and Vancouver and all points east. And the daily local milk run from Ruby Creek to Vancouver and back mustn't be forgotten. The railway's facilities eventually grew to the point where there was a ninety-two-car siding and a 142-car yard. In fact, prosperity and prospects were such that Mission narrowly escaped being renamed "New Seattle" in 1899! By 1909 the volume of both passenger traffic and local freight was such that a new station had to be built.

This second station was a prefabricated structure manufactured by the BC Mills Timber and Trading Company of Vancouver. This firm, which grew out of the original Hastings Mill, produced a variety of designs for both residential and commercial buildings between 1904 and 1911. The station pictured arrived from Vancouver as a "kit" to be assembled by local builders.

The building was a typical "second-generation" station, providing more space and amenities than did the minimum facilities contained in the twenty-three-year-old first station. On the main floor there was a general waiting room, a ladies' room, a baggage room, and the station master's office, with its bay window giving a clear view up and down the track. On the second floor was the apartment provided for the station agent and his family. The exterior of the building presented an English-cottage look, with its half-timbered decoration in the bracketed gables. The shingle siding, however, betrayed the structure's West Coast origin. Wide overhanging eaves supported by heavy ornamented brackets not only gave the station charm, but also provided passengers with necessary shelter from the elements. The station remained in use until 1990.

Current plans call for the building to be moved to a site facing Highway Number 7 on the eastern edge of Mission. There it is to serve as home for Mission's Travel and Business Information Office. Space will also be provided for the Chamber of Commerce and for the Mission Kinsmen Club. The Kinsmen have provided leadership in the local campaign to save the station from demolition. Unfortunately, the unused building was severely damaged by fire in October 1993. While the exterior could be salvaged, the interior was beyond restoration.

CROSSING THE RIVER

U ntil the completion of the BC Electric's interurban line to Chilliwack on October 3, 1910, communities on the south side of the Fraser River had no direct or convenient route to New Westminster and Vancouver. They could travel the slow and rough Yale Road by horse and wagon, or they could board one of the sternwheelers that made the return trip from New Westminster twice a week. For those living around Chilliwack, another option (after 1886) was to cross the Fraser River to Harrison Mills, where they could board the CPR transcontinental train en route to Vancouver.

Crossing the river wasn't as easy as it sounds. Before 1901 it meant rowing or canoeing from one shore to the other. Beginning in the winter of 1887-88, there was a regular canoe service of sorts. J.T. Harrison held a federal contract to operate a ferry service and to provide mail delivery between the CPR line at Harrison Mills and Chilliwack. In 1899 this contract passed to William MacDonald, who carried both passengers and mail by canoe until July 1, 1901, when he was drowned during a freshet.

This tragedy sparked demand for a less hazardous crossing. Captain William Menten and J.F. Harrison responded and soon put into operation the *Minto,* a sixty-foot long sternwheeler with a twelve-foot beam, which was licensed to carry twenty passengers. This new service was also subsidized by a federal mail contract. Menten and Harrison's *Minto* continued in service until June 1908, when they sold out to Captain J.T. Henley, Captain James Garvey, and A.E. Yates. This trio put a new boat, the *J.P. Douglas,* on the run that summer and operated as the Chilliwack Ferry Service.

The *J.P. Douglas,* ninety feet long with a twenty-six-foot beam, was in service only eight months before it burned and sank while locked in ice at the mouth of the Harrison River. The engines were salvaged and used in a new vessel, the *Vedder,* which was put into service in May 1909. Smaller than the *Douglas,* at seventy-five feet long with a twenty-two-foot beam, the *Vedder* made two daily crossings between Chilliwack and Harrison Mills. The ship lay overnight at Chilliwack Landing and left in the morning in time to meet the west-bound train and in the evening in time to meet the east-bound train. In addition to passengers, mail, and express, freight was carried as required. When they were in season fruit crops were transported across the river for rail shipment to the Prairies. Even livestock, on occasion, made the trip across the Fraser.

With the awarding of the mail contract to the BC Electric in 1911, the *Vedder* was taken off the run and moved to Hope to serve as a ferry until the combined rail and highway bridge across the Fraser opened in 1914. A smaller motor boat continued to provide a regular service between Harrison Mills and Chilliwack until 1920.

TALLY-HO!

Pictured at the Hollow Tree in Stanley Park is the Stanley Park Livery Stable's tally-ho. Even in the Edwardian era, no dedicated tourists worth their salt would visit Vancouver without going to Stanley Park. A number of livery companies routinely picked up passengers at the major hotels for the drive around the park perimeter. The fare was a dollar per person.

Stanley Park Livery Stables stood at the corner of Seymour and Dunsmuir. The livery business involved more than providing sight-seeing trips for visitors. The company advertised "forty rigs, seven hacks, and two tally-hos." Furthermore, the stable boarded horses for both businesses and individuals, and it operated a "sales stable where a fine class of horseflesh is dealt in, and where many of the most important horse deals of the city are consummated."

One was also informed in the advertising that "impressions of Vancouver – the 'Sunset City' – will be made all the more lasting by seeing the City in a comfortable Hack, Brougham, Surrey, Victoria, or Tally-ho." For those who need a quick course in carriage recognition, the following may be helpful. A *hack* is any light four-wheeled cart with one or more seats; a *brougham* is a one-horse closed carriage with two or four wheels; and a *surrey* is an American four-wheeled two-seated pleasure vehicle with both seats facing forward. The *victoria* is by far the most elegant vehicle. It is a light, low, four-wheeled carriage with a collapsible hood, with seating for two people and an elevated seat in front for the driver. Another local firm advertised "Handsome Victorias, 'liveried drivers,' very suitable for ladies calling and driving." The victoria was the ideal vehicle for seeing and for being seen! A *tally-ho* is a large four-in-hand that can carry a good number of people. Vancouver Transfer advertised its "rubber-tyred *tally-ho*" as accommodating thirty people.

By 1909 times were changing; the day of the horse-drawn vehicle was coming to an end. Stanley Park Stables advertised that "one of its two *tally-hos* was an automobile," and Vancouver Transfer was inviting tourists to "Ride on the Big Red Auto." Both firms could read the writing on the wall as far as the livery business was concerned. In 1909, while there were still eleven livery stables in the city, there were already fifteen auto salesrooms and repair shops.

Some things have changed over the years; tally-hos have all but been replaced by sight-seeing buses. At the same time, much remains the same; visitors still circle Stanley Park and stop for picture-taking at the Hollow Tree. Regardless of when or how one first drives around the park, the beauty of the trees, the wonder of the harbour, and the splendour of the city's mountain backdrop cannot fail to impress any newcomer to the "Sunset City."

CHRIST CHURCH CATHEDRAL

In 1888 there was only one Anglican Church in Vancouver – St. James's at the corner of Gore and Cordova. St. James's was in the High Church or Anglo-Catholic tradition, with much ritual and ceremony marking its services. Some parishioners, who had come from a Low Church or Evangelical tradition, asked the bishop to form a parish "that was distinctively to uphold the principles of the Reformation and of the Evangelical Ministry." The bishop agreed to do so, and the first services of the new congregation were held in 1888 in a meeting room on Seymour Street.

In August 1888, land on the northeast corner of Georgia and Burrard was bought from the CPR for $2,500 for the new parish of Christ Church. It was decided that a stone church should be built at a cost not to exceed $25,000. The English-born architect C. Osborne Wickenden was commissioned to prepare plans. While working on a design for Christ Church, Wickenden was also preparing plans for the first Vancouver Club building (at Hastings and Hornby) and for the city's first permanent post office (at Pender and Granville). His design for a church, "in the early Gothic style," was accepted by the parish in March 1889.

Initially, only the granite-walled basement was completed, providing temporary space for a congregation of 500. The basement cost $6,000, which was all the money that was available at the time. It was another five years before the church proper could be built. The incomplete building, something of an eyesore (it was nicknamed "the Rootcellar"), didn't please the CPR, who felt the unsightly structure was holding up the sale of valuable adjoining lots. Things got going again in July 1894, and by February 1895 the building, an enlarged version of the one originally planned, was completed. The church could seat just under 900 people.

By the early 1900s, the growth of the West End had made Christ Church the largest Anglican parish in Western Canada, and more seating space was needed. W.T. Dalton drew up plans that called for lengthening the chancel and widening the transepts in order to increase seating by 400. While his plan also called for small galleries that could accommodate a further 400 people, these were never built. And they were not the only thing that was never built. Wickenden's original design called for a 140-foot spire rising above the main entrance. It can be assumed that the main reason the spire was never built was cost. When the renovations were completed in 1910, Christ Church became the largest Anglican church west of Toronto.

The picture shows the building shortly after it was enlarged. It was not until 1929 that Christ Church was selected to be the cathedral of the Diocese of New Westminster, replacing the Royal City's Holy Trinity, which had been named as cathedral in 1892. Christ Church is not only the first stone church built in Vancouver, it is also the city's oldest surviving church building.

"Temples Of Commerce"

Edwardians had a healthy respect for money and an inordinate regard for those who had lots of it! Their respect for money as the measure of all things found architectural expression in the Neo-Classical banks. Vancouver's first temple bank was built in 1903 by the Royal Bank at Hastings and Homer. Soon after, the Bank of Commerce acquired both a prime site and an outstanding design for its temple bank three blocks west at Hastings and Granville. The building was designed by Darling and Pearson, Toronto architects who later worked on the Parliament Buildings in Ottawa after they had been severely damaged by fire. The bank opened on December 21, 1908.

By 1914 there were sixteen different banks in Vancouver. The first to open had been the Bank of British Columbia and the Bank of Montreal in 1886. There were banks with names like Molson's, Merchants, Northern Crown, Union, and Traders. There were also banks whose very names suggested empire, like the Imperial, Dominion, and Standard. And then there were banks whose names identified their roots, like the Banks of Ottawa, Hamilton, Toronto, Nova Scotia, Quebec, Eastern Townships, and even Vancouver. Most of these banks no longer exist, having amalgamated with Canada's "big five" banks. Two of them simply failed.

Today, when banks go out of their way to appear to be user-friendly, it's difficult to imagine just how intimidating a visit to the bank might have been seventy-five years ago. There were no coffee urns, no cookies for customers, no balloons, no candies, and certainly no tellers dressed in costumes on Halloween! Cavernous banking halls of marble, oak, and brass were the order of the day. They were designed to inspire awe, wonder, and fear in the hearts of would-be borrowers. These temples of commerce were served by an all-knowing male priesthood. Laypeople were encouraged to think of the bank manager as someone of unfailing wisdom and judgement, a veritable oracle when it came to money matters. Such women as there were in the banks formed a kind of fiscal altar guild. They could *never, never* aspire to be anything more than stenographers or cleaning women.

The *Greater Vancouver Illustrated* of 1909 states that "there is no trust more sacred than that of the bank ... That those at the head of the institutions are of more than average acumen is proved by the number of banks ... that are profitable and prosperous ... The bank managers' virtue was further confirmed by the fact that they exercised the greatest conservatism ... in the lending of money on real-estate and commercial ventures." Probably most bank managers of the day would have agreed with Robert Dunsmuir's belief that "property is the standard of intelligence." This conservatism continued to find expression in bank architecture. Long after the rest of the business community had abandoned the glories of Greek and Roman architecture as a way of making a corporate statement, the banks continued to build "temples of commerce" as symbols of what they imagined to be their enduring strength and power.

BIRKS – PARADISE LOST

For those who grew up in Vancouver between the grand opening of Birks and Sons' new store on November 10, 1913, and its demolition in 1974, it was *the* store. It epitomized style, elegance, and luxury. Located at Georgia and Granville, Henry Birks and Sons' store, with its spaciousness, elaborately decorated plaster ceiling, "Empire" chandeliers, mahogany panelling, lighted display cases, and terrazzo floors, (with areas carpeted in rich *Birks blue)* managed to make shopping an event, if not a quasi-religious experience! The staff, immaculately turned out in suitably subdued costume, made everyone, from millionaire to milliner, feel welcome, important, and special.

Birks and Sons' had come to Vancouver in 1906 when it bought out Trorey's (Vancouver's most prestigious jeweller and watch maker) at Hastings and Granville. On July 2, 1912, the company received a building permit to erect its new building at Granville and Georgia. The building not only provided space for the Birks store, but also for ten storeys of offices. It was designed by Somervell and Putnam, a Seattle firm that did some significant work in Vancouver. Built at a cost of $1,250,000, the Birks Building came to be regarded as the city's finest pre-First World War building. There are still many Vancouverites who remember with real regret the building's demolition in the mid-seventies.

THE VANCOUVER BLOCK

It is ironic that the much-admired Birks Building fell victim to the wreckers ball, while the rather plain Vancouver Block survived the downtown redevelopment surge of the 1970s. The Vancouver Block was built for Dominic Burns, brother of Calgary meat packer Senator Pat Burns. Designed by Parr, MacKenzie and Day, the building opened August 21, 1912, providing space for 350 offices, two ground-floor stores, a restaurant, and a penthouse apartment (for its owner). The Commercial Club was the name of the top-floor restaurant, where, in 1912, a full-course luncheon, "beautifully served," cost fifty cents.

Without doubt, the building's chief claim to fame is its clock. The four faces are twenty-two feet in diameter, and the glass protecting each face is seven-eighths of an inch thick and weighs four tons. The minute hands are eleven feet long, and the hour hands eight feet. The clock was built by the Standard Electric Time Company of San Francisco for slightly more than $10,000. When installed, the Vancouver Block's clock was the largest in Canada. While once the clock could be seen from virtually any point in Vancouver, today, towering neighbours have almost hidden the huge timepiece from view.

Vancouver's Opera House

One of the amenities promised those who bought lots in the CPR's exclusive West End was a convenient first-class theatre. For a time it seemed that this promise was not going to be fulfilled. To the relief of the city's patricians, however, work began on the theatre in February 1890. It was located on Granville Street, next to the first Hotel Vancouver, and cost over $200,000. The Vancouver Opera House, as it was called, was designed by an as yet unidentified architect. Given its nondescript appearance, his anonymity may be his just reward; even by Victorian standards of popular taste, the opera house was an incredibly ugly building, both inside and out.

The auditorium seated 1,550 in boxes, dress-circle stalls, and a second balcony. Orchestra-floor patrons seated under the dress circle could have their view of the stage partially blocked by one of six posts that supported the lower balcony. The stage was 150 feet wide and forty-three feet deep. The building's only feature that consistently got rave reviews was the drop screen or fire curtain that featured a "magnificent world famous painting in oil of the mountains known as the Three Sisters and the Bow River at Banff, Alberta." It was painted in New York and was brought to Vancouver on two flatcars (one not being long enough). The exaggerated sensibilities of the day were not neglected: there were separate box offices for "Ladies" and "Gents" on opposite sides of the entrance foyer.

Opening night was February 9, 1891. Wagner's *Lohengrin* was presented by the Juch Grand Opera Company, a troupe that travelled the United States, Canada, and Mexico between 1885 and 1891. The company was the creation of Emma Juch, a soprano of considerable talent. She was noted for her impeccable diction and her wide vocal range. While it is not known whether *Lohengrin* was sung in German or in English, we do know that Emma Juch was an early champion of opera being performed in English. Regardless of whether it was in German, English, or even Esperanto, it is hard to imagine a Vancouver audience of 1891 really being all that keen on Wagner!

Managed by the CPR's land department, the Vancouver Opera House was a great success. The fact that, until 1898, it was the only theatre in town worthy of the name guaranteed this. During the 1890s, even the BC Electric tried to accommodate those at the opera. While streetcars normally stopped running at 11:00 PM, on opera nights they were held outside the theatre until the performance ended.

The last performance at the Vancouver Opera House took place on July 9, 1911. The building was sold to a Seattle-based theatre circuit controlled by T.D. Sullivan and J.W. Considine. After extensive remodelling, the theatre reopened on March 17, 1913, as the New Orpheum and featured the finest vaudeville of the day. Over time the theatre was called the Orpheum, the Vancouver, the Lyric, the International Cinema, and once again, the Lyric before it was torn down in 1969 to make way for the first phase of the Pacific Centre complex – the Eaton's store and the Toronto-Dominion Bank tower.

An Edwardian Street Scene

Depicting Edwardian Vancouver, the picture before you shows Hastings Street looking east from Howe Street, although it could easily pass for some English provincial city of the same era. You might think of Birmingham, Leeds, or Sheffield, for example. And Vancouver's architects, builders, and city fathers would have been both delighted and flattered by your mistake! By 1911 Vancouver was fast becoming a British city. Some 30 per cent of the population was born in Great Britain, a considerable change from 1901, when only 15 per cent were from the "Old Country."

Both the Winch Building and the post office, with its elaborate clock tower, reflected the best in Edwardian architecture. The post office, which was built between 1905 and 1910, was designed by Public Works staff, and its anonymous architects deserve full marks for their Edwardian Baroque creation. Its neighbour to the immediate west, the Winch Building, has to be regarded as one of the city's most beautiful office buildings. It cost R.V. Winch $700,000 to build it in 1908-09. Winch had made a fortune in salmon canneries and sawmills and lived in high style: he would have neither built nor owned a building that was anything but first class.

In today's jargon, Winch lucked out. The architect he chose was Thomas Hooper, who is one of the two architects who have been held "responsible for the majority of nondescript commercial buildings that were constructed during the boom years of the late nineteenth and early twentieth century." Fortunately not all his buildings were without character. Hooper did have bright moments, and none was more so than the one that led him to develop his plan for the Winch Building – the first commercial building west of Granville and one of the city's last significant structures to be named after its owner. It was probably one of the finest buildings produced by Hooper's firm.

Hooper undoubtedly got the idea for his ground-floor arched windows from the adjacent post office building. One suspects he also borrowed the colonnettes and pediment that identify the main entrance to the Winch Building from the post office's clock tower. The similarities between the two buildings are such that even today many people mistakenly assume that both were built to be parts of a federal post office complex. To give Hooper credit, however, his scale was such that it neither overpowered the post office nor allowed it to lessen the significance of his own structure. It is hard to find fault with either building. The post office represents the best of Edwardian "public-works" architecture, and the Winch Building reflects Edwardian commercial architecture at its finest.

Happily, both the post office and the Winch Building have been preserved. They are component parts of the Sinclair Centre and, as such, have a new and well-deserved lease on life.

When Lacrosse Was Big

At the turn of the century Stanley Park's Brockton Point was home to many sports, including lacrosse. Lacrosse came late to BC. The British had brought cricket and rugby around the Horn with them, and the Americans had brought baseball and basketball north in their carpet-bags before lacrosse arrived on the local scene. Lacrosse, which was the biggest team sport in Ontario and Quebec at the time of Confederation, made its way west with the CPR in the 1880s. Newly arrived Easterners soon popularized the sport locally.

A.E. "Bony" Suckling put together a Vancouver team and organized the first game between Vancouver and Victoria. It took place in Victoria on the twenty-fourth of May weekend in 1888. Vancouver won. A return match was scheduled for the Dominion Day holiday in Vancouver, and this time Victoria won. In the late 1880s lacrosse clubs had been formed in Victoria, Vancouver, and New Westminster, and in 1890 the Amateur Lacrosse Association came into being. In the 1890s rivalries grew intense. By then New Westminster had a team – and what a team! Proudly bearing what was originally a derisive nickname given them by the Vancouver team and its fans, the *New Westminster Salmonbellies* was the team to beat for most of the early amateur (and later professional) years of lacrosse on the West Coast. As the best professional lacrosse team in Canada, the *Salmonbellies* won the Minto Cup every year but one from 1908 until 1924. While even the top teams were technically amateur until 1905, each brought in experienced players from Ontario with promises of high-paying jobs and cash prizes for wins. In those days, so long as a player wasn't trying to make a living exclusively from his sport, he was considered an amateur. Times were different back then!

Lacrosse was not a game for the weak. Both players and spectators expected a certain number of dust-ups on the field as part of every game. Even without fights, lacrosse was a tough game. Players went out to play without helmets or face masks and, until the teams turned professional, without either gloves or pads. The last professional Minto Cup game was played in 1924. A number of reasons have been given for the demise of lacrosse. While excessive violence may have been a factor, a more likely explanation is the family car. Lacrosse was a summer sport, and with the coming of the automobile people had other things to do with a sunny Saturday afternoon than go to lacrosse games.

Lacrosse had a brief reprieve of sorts in the 1930s. Professional ice hockey, like lacrosse, had left Vancouver in the mid-1920s. This meant that the Patrick family's Vancouver Arena at Denman and Georgia was looking for tenants. Box lacrosse, an indoor version of the game, had been developed in Ontario in 1932, and in 1933 it became a regular attraction at the arena in Vancouver. Teams like the *Richmond Farmers* and the *North Shore Indians* were playing older teams like the *Salmonbellies,* which had reverted to amateur status. All went well until August 19, 1936, when the arena burned to the ground. Essentially, it was "game over" for lacrosse as a major spectator sport in Vancouver. Since 1937, each year the Minto Cup has been presented to the winning junior championship team.

Seraphim "Joe" Fortes

The message on the back of the picture postcard that appears with this article begins, "This is the man that learnt the children to swim. His name is Joe." It was mailed from Vancouver to Tonopah, Nevada, on July 29, 1907. As usual, Joe Fortes is surrounded by children as he dives into the water in this scene at English Bay. Three sources variously report Joe Fortes's birthplace as Jamaica, Trinidad, and Barbados, respectively. We'll play it safe, and just say that Seraphim "Joe" Fortes started life in the West Indies. He was probably born around 1860, although, like his place of birth, his date of birth is more than a little uncertain.

In his youth he went to sea, sailing before the mast on British windjammers. In 1883 he left Glasgow on the *Robert Kerr,* which finally reached Vancouver via Cape Horn in 1885. While in Vancouver, the vessel was declared unseaworthy and prohibited from returning to the high seas. In 1886 it was sold to the CPR and converted into a coal barge. This left Joe Fortes high and dry. He must have been ready to settle down, however, for it wasn't long before he had built himself a little house far from the city, down at English Bay. He was almost the only inhabitant of the area.

Even in the late 1880s though, there were children finding their way along the forest paths to the beach to play and swim. Fortes, who was an expert swimmer, took charge of the kids at the beach. Doubtless his exceptional size, unfamiliar colour, and warm and winning manner made him a figure to be respected and obeyed. In something over thirty years he taught literally thousands of Vancouver children to swim. He was always a wise and kindly guardian, and a highly competent "natural" teacher. Finally, in September 1900, Fortes was hired by the city to do what he had been doing voluntarily for the past ten years. He became Vancouver's first paid lifeguard and swimming instructor, and the English Bay Constable.

By the time he died, on February 4, 1922, he was possibly Vancouver's most popular citizen and certainly its best recognized. As it was expressed in his obituary, "The death of the old coloured lifeguard whose constant vigil and unselfish devotion to duty kept many a family circle unbroken, will throw a spirit of sadness into almost every Vancouver home." "Old Joe" was taken to the Vancouver General Hospital with pneumonia, which developed into mumps. While in the hospital he died of a paralytic stroke.

His funeral at Holy Rosary Cathedral and burial at Mountain View Cemetery were paid for by the city in appreciation of his life of service to Vancouver and its children. Today, a West End library and restaurant bear his name. As well, a memorial drinking fountain (commissioned by the Kiwanis Club, designed by Charles Marega, and paid for by public subscription) still stands near English Bay in Alexandra Park. The granite and polished bronze memorial was unveiled on February 15, 1926. The inscription reads, "The Children Loved Him." What more could anyone ask?

VANCOUVER HIGH SCHOOL

When school reopened after the Christmas holidays on January 6, 1890, there were enough older students to form Vancouver's first high-school class. A room was provided in Central School, located on Pender between Cambie and Hamilton. By September of the same year, enrolment was such that the high-school students had to be moved into a two-room annex on the Central School grounds. By 1893 there were sufficient pupils of high-school age to warrant building the eight-room brick Vancouver High School on the northwest corner of Dunsmuir and Cambie. Within a decade this building, too, was bursting at the seams.

In the summer of 1903, the Vancouver School Board bought seven acres south of False Creek for $6,500. The property, covering two city blocks, was bounded by Oak and Laurel Streets, and Tenth and Twelfth Avenues. The building erected on this Fairview site in 1904 was the new Vancouver High School. It replaced the building on Dunsmuir, which became, in turn, the Vancouver School Board offices and the Vancouver School of Art. The new stone structure had twenty classrooms as well as an auditorium on the top floor that could seat 700 people. The science room was considered to be the most up-to-date in Canada, and the commercial department not only had twelve typewriters, but also a rotary mimeograph and letter files. When the new building was opened on January 5, 1905, over a thousand people came to see the beautiful new high school for themselves. This pictured lithograph dates from the time of the school's opening.

By 1908, the new high school was already too small. While a new wing facing Twelfth Avenue was planned in order to provide a dozen additional classrooms, the school board decided that there was a need for a second high school on the east side of town. Two high schools meant, of course, that each had to have its own name. On August 24, 1908, the name "King Edward," for "Edward VII, the Peace Maker," was recommended for the old Vancouver High School, and the name "Britannia," for "the symbol of the Mother Country, respected and loved," was recommended for the new east-end high school. On May 24, 1910, what had been Vancouver High School officially became King Edward High School. Two years later, it got its new wing of twelve classrooms, offices, and a new auditorium.

King Edward High School closed in 1962, when it was replaced by Eric Hamber Secondary School, which had been built at 33rd and Oak. In the 1960s the old school building was renovated and became the centre for a continuing education program that eventually developed into what is now known as Vancouver Community College, with its numerous campuses and great variety of programs.

Had the school board ever wondered what it would eventually do with the old building, its problem was solved on June 19, 1973, when it burned down. All that remains today of what was originally Vancouver High School, and later King Edward High School, are parts of the ornamental stone wall that bordered the Twelfth Avenue side of the old school grounds.

Capilano's Canyon View Hotel

Capilano Canyon has been a popular place for Vancouverites to visit since the city's early days. Its natural beauty made it an attractive destination for city folk who wanted to explore the back and beyond, but who generally could travel no farther than the streetcar and their feet could carry them. In the 1900s two small hotels opened on the Capilano River and were immediately popular. One was Pete Larson's Canyon View Hotel. It was only a few yards upstream from the great chasm of the Second Canyon, now the site of Cleveland Dam.

Opened in May 1909, the hotel, pictured here in its heyday, provided first-class accommodation. Contemporary newspapers detailed its attractions. They spoke of the reception room, which featured high wainscotting and a large granite fireplace, and of the dining room, "which for size and general appointments compared favourably with that of ... the best mountain hotels in the Province." And they naturally had to let the world know that the kitchen was "fitted with a large Gurney range and with every convenience of a modern culinary department." Readers were also told of the main-floor sitting room and of the bar, which was beyond the office safely out of sight of the ladies but doubtless in full view of the hotel manager. Reports went on to say that on the second and third floors were thirty rooms, a ladies' parlour, and three suites, all "tastefully furnished and fitted with hot air registers." Lighting for the whole building was provided "by means of powerful gasoline lamps which gave off a soft and brilliant light."

Larson, who owned and had successfully operated the North Vancouver Hotel on Esplanade for many years, was ahead of his time when it came to public relations. When the Canyon View Hotel was opening, he invited the members of both the North Vancouver District Council and the North Vancouver City Council for a special tour of the building and dinner. The dinner was followed by toasts to: "The King and Empire," "Canada and the Federal and Provincial Governments," "City and District of North Vancouver," "The Industries of North Vancouver," "The Pioneer Reeves of the District," "The Mayor of the City," "The Present District Officials," and "The Ladies."

Larson continued to operate the hotel until 1928, when it was sold to Sunset Holdings, who opened the Second Canyon suspension bridge on July second of the same year. While there was already a suspension bridge lower down the Capilano River at the First Canyon, the new bridge was more impressive. It was 250 feet long and, being 425 feet above the river, was claimed to be the highest suspension bridge in the world. In 1930 the hotel again changed hands. Even though the new owner spent $25,000 on renovations, nothing could save it from the effects of the Depression. After it had served for a time as a girls' school, the building's final role was as a bunkhouse for workers building Cleveland Dam. The old Canyon View Hotel was torn down in 1952, the year after the suspension bridge had been dismantled. When Cleveland Dam was completed, the "canyon view" was very different from what it had been in 1909 when Pete Larson chose the name for his hotel on the Capilano.

THE EMPIRE'S TALLEST BUILDING

Our picture has a typical Vancouver winter's-day quality about it: no leaves on the trees beside the old court house, no mountains visible beyond the north end of Cambie Street, and a light that seems to have passed through a grey filter. The tall building on the northwest corner of Hastings and Cambie is the thirteen-storey Dominion Building. When it opened in March 1910, it was the tallest building in the British Empire and soon to be at the centre of a local financial debacle.

The building was originally the creation of Imperial Trust, one of over thirty trust companies operating in Vancouver at that time. The city was home to a small army of would-be financiers and land speculators. Real estate agencies outnumbered grocers three to one. Imperial Trust had stretched its resources to the limit to finance the building and, finding itself on the verge of collapse, hastily arranged a merger with another Vancouver-based company, Dominion Trust. By 1913 Dominion Trust was also in financial difficulty and, to save itself, sold the controlling interest in the new building to the Dominion Bank. The sale of the building only managed to postpone the inevitable. On October 12, 1914, Dominion Trust's managing director shot himself, and on October 23 the bankrupt company went into liquidation. Contributing to the company's difficulty was the fact that the dead man had made heavy and unauthorized loans without the knowledge and consent of the directors. The liquidators could only conclude that "five million dollars had disappeared into thin air." Shareholders ended up with about thirty cents on the dollar.

The Dominion Building, Vancouver's first skyscraper, provided some 260 offices above the ground floor. Each floor had its own fire hydrant, and the building was advertised as absolutely fireproof. Unique among office buildings of the time was the absence of a light well; all windows were outside windows. Designed by J.S. Helyer, the structure was of steel and concrete, faced in red brick and ochre terracotta. From its Classical columns flanking the main entrance to its French mansard roof, the building was a stylistic mish-mash, and it received mixed reactions.

In its early years the Dominion Building's offices didn't rent well. Would-be tenants didn't care for its odd-shaped offices and unusual floor plan, which featured a central core with a ten-storey spiral staircase! Nowadays, however, it almost always enjoys full occupancy. The Dominion Bank sold the building in 1943 to S.J. Cohen, owner of the Army and Navy Department Store. He bought the building with the idea of turning it into a department store at the end of the Second World War but, somewhere along the way, changed his mind. The Cohen family maintained the building beautifully over the years, and it stands today as a superbly preserved monument to an era of overreaching ambition – an era when a popular slogan insisted: "Many Men Making Money Means Much For Vancouver."

THE EXHIBITION

When, in 1889, Vancouver acquired a 160-acre land grant from the province in the east side of the city, it was intended that the land retain much of its wilderness state and be, in many ways, a smaller version of the 950-acre Stanley Park. Almost immediately, however, the Jockey Club got both permission and financial aid to build a racetrack in the new Hastings Park, as it was called. The track was nothing grand, just a country course that was nineteen feet lower at one end than it was at the other, encircling an oval of stumps and forest debris. It hadn't improved all that much when the Vancouver Exhibition Association entered the picture in 1908.

The Board of Management of this new association chose Hastings Park as its preferred site for what it hoped would become an annual fair. There was some objection from the racing fraternity and a lot of opposition from the powers behind the old established annual fair in New Westminster. Not surprisingly, Premier McBride opposed the establishment of a competing fair and made it quite clear that the provincial government would not provide any financial assistance. The fact that he was born and bred in New Westminster may have coloured his thinking.

Opposition didn't discourage those backing the idea of a Vancouver Exhibition. There was one very practical argument for an exhibition in Vancouver: going to New Westminster involved a trip either on the CPR or on the BC Electric interurban, and this trip was expensive, both in time and in money. Those arguing for an exhibition in Vancouver could remind the voters that all it would take to get to the fair would be a five-cent streetcar ride. Their logic prevailed, and voters approved a $50,000 by-law.

Designed by Henry Watson, the building typified fair buildings being erected everywhere on the continent. It was 240 feet long, 100 feet wide, and had verandas on both the ground and first floors. There was an interior balcony seventeen feet wide encircling the main floor. Plans called for a "ladies' tearoom" at the east end of the balcony and a "fairy fountain with fairy lights playing on water jets" in the centre of the main floor. The two circular ends of the white and gold building were of glass, and its final cost was $36,964.

Unfortunately, the exhibition building wasn't completed in time for a fair to be held in 1909. The grand opening had to wait until August 16, 1910. And grand it was. The prime minister, Sir Wilfred Laurier, came to perform the opening ceremonies. That was enough to guarantee the attendance of every Liberal in town. It was also enough to move Premier McBride to write to the president of the Exhibition Association, extending his best wishes for the success of the fair and enclosing his Conservative government's cheque for $10,000! The exhibition was an immediate triumph, with 68,000 attending in the first year. The Vancouver Exhibition's first building, seen beyond the old-growth stumps and few remaining trees in Hastings Park, was demolished in 1939.

Vancouver's Most Elegant Building

In 1912 Francis Swales, a leading New York architect, was hired by the CPR to design a new Hotel Vancouver. It was to be built on the Granville and Georgia site, which, since 1886, had been occupied by the first Hotel Vancouver. Swales's job was not an easy one. Not only did he have to incorporate two earlier wings built along Howe Street – one designed by Francis Rattenbury, the other by Walter Painter – but he also had to design a structure that could be built without necessitating the hotel's closure for even a single day. Somehow he managed it, postponing the demolition of the old hotel until 1914, by which time the new facilities were sufficiently in place to allow the business to continue without interruption.

Working for the CPR was not all that easy. In 1906, Rattenbury had complained that there were "few fixed, and many constantly changing ideas on the part of the head of the company's hotel system." In 1912 Swales was initially expected to work in partnership with Painter, who had been the railway's chief architect for seven years. The partnership only lasted a short time before Swales was allowed to get on with the job by himself. And he was very successful. The CPR had decreed its new hotel was to be in the Renaissance style, and, even though the building's exterior was decorated by larger-than-life sculptured buffalo heads, it somehow managed to reflect the grandeur of fifteenth-century Tuscany. The second hotel was probably the most sumptuous building ever built in Vancouver. The public rooms were richly decorated and vast. In fact, everything about the hotel was big. The bar was 100 feet long, the billiard room had 10 tables, the barber shop had 16 chairs, and there were 6 ornate passenger elevators. The hotel also claimed to have the largest cookstove in the world. There were 650 guest rooms and a staff of 520.

Swales's Hotel Vancouver opened its doors in July 1916. It had cost over twelve million dollars to build, yet, incredibly, it stayed open for only twenty-three years. There was, of course, a reason: the Depression. The CPR's rival, the CNR, had been building a new hotel at Georgia and Burrard since 1928. The Depression had forced the CNR to halt work on its new hotel more than once for lack of money. Since the CPR was also facing an economic pinch, the CNR suggested that the new hotel be operated jointly, and the former agreed. One condition of the deal was that the CPR close its "old" hotel.

Eventually, the CPR's Hotel Vancouver closed its doors in 1939, when the present Hotel Vancouver opened in time for the visit of King George VI and Queen Elizabeth, now the Queen Mother. The old hotel was used by the military during the Second World War and as a residence for veterans and their families immediately afterwards. The building was bought by the T. Eaton Company in 1948. Despite the protests of the Architectural Institute of BC, the Vancouver Tourist Association, and the Vancouver Board of Trade, the building was torn down in 1949. After serving as a parking lot for twenty years, Eaton's built its present store on the site. Had the old Hotel Vancouver survived into our own time, it would probably be internationally regarded as one of the world's great hotels.

SALMON CANNING ON THE FRASER

Our picture dates from around 1905. A tug and a scow loaded with salmon have arrived at a New Westminster cannery from the fishing grounds at the mouth of the Fraser River. The four men in the scow are unloading the fish onto the cannery's roofed wharf, where they will be hosed down to remove dirt and slime and moved out of the sun to keep their flesh firm. While it was preferable that fish be canned within twenty-four hours of being caught, they were still usable for up to forty-eight hours.

The canneries got their fish from both independent fishers under contract and from their own fleet of boats, which were operated by hired fishers. While contract fishers were paid a certain amount per fish, those employed directly by the canneries were paid on the basis of a twelve-hour day. There could be as many as 2,000 skiffs gill-netting at the mouth of the Fraser at any one time. Unless the run was very poor, only sockeye would ever get to the canneries, which set daily maximums for the number of fish they would buy from individual fishers. In off years coho might be canned, but until 1911 sockeye was the main stock canned for export. While two people gill-netting from a skiff have been known to catch more than 1,000 fish in one night, the usual catch was between 100 and 500 fish per two-person crew.

Fraser River salmon were first shipped overseas in the 1830s. The Hudson's Bay Company packed salted salmon in barrels and shipped it first to Hawaii and Asia and, later, to the American east coast and Europe. Salmon were first canned successfully on the Sacramento River in California. In 1867, James Symes became the first person on the Fraser to successfully preserve cooked salmon in hermetically sealed tins. The first commercial cannery on the Fraser was opened by Alexander Loggie and Company in June 1870 at Annieville, about three miles downstream from New Westminster.

Day or night, as a tug with its scow full of salmon approached the wharf, a blast of the cannery whistle brought the workers, all of whom lived nearby, running. Nearly all the labour, male and female, were non-White. European immigrants and those who had moved to BC from Eastern Canada and the U.S. were more inclined to try their luck at logging or mining than at working in a salmon cannery. Chinese and Native workers were recruited by local Chinese labour contractors, who paid them on a piecework basis.

The work could be both tiring and boring, so workers created their own distractions. In his *Above the Sandheads,* Ellis Ladner tells us that men tossing fish from the scow to the wharf – like those in our picture – would make wagers on their ability to land the fish on a certain spot. The tedious work and twelve-hour days never lasted for long. The peak salmon run only lasted a week, and a cannery's season, including time both to prepare for the run and to clean up after it, would not have been more than two or three months.

THE *PRINCESS VICTORIA*

Beginning in 1825, for thirty-seven years the ships of the Hudson's Bay Company provided a connecting link between the various ports on the Pacific coast. In 1862, Captain William Irving of New Westminster provided an alternate choice for travellers and shippers with his Pioneer Line. These two competitors joined forces in 1883 to form the Canadian Pacific Navigation (CPN) Company.

While the CPR's William Van Horne wanted to establish a coastal service of his own as early as 1886, the railway's uncertain finances forced him to settle for a contractual agreement with CPN that lasted for the next fifteen years. As the new century approached, dissatisfaction with CPN's service was commonplace, and in 1898 the Victoria Board of Trade went so far as to ask the CPR to provide a coastal service. Van Horne, who was not one to abandon a dream quickly (especially a potentially profitable one), welcomed the invitation. Coincidentally, the Hudson's Bay Company wanted to sell its CPN shares and lobbied other CPN shareholders to do the same. On January 12, 1901, the CPR acquired all CPN shares for $531,000.

The first new vessel built for the CPR's coastal steamship service was at once the fastest and finest on the Coast. The *Princess Victoria*, pictured at the CPR's wharf in Vancouver, was originally intended to be a paddle steamer. However, to allow for use on the Alaska run, a propeller-driven vessel was deemed the better choice. Launched on November 18, 1902, at Newcastle-on-Tyne, the *Princess Victoria* arrived on the Pacific coast 130 days later. That summer, old speed records fell regularly, and in late August it made the crossing from Victoria to Vancouver in under three and a half hours! With tall stacks and open decks, it was very much up-to-date; spartan furnishing and cramped cabins were a thing of the past. There were even four large staterooms with private baths. The *Princess Victoria*'s speed made a new and unprecedented service possible in 1904. Carrying a double crew, the ship could make the 325-mile trip from Victoria to Vancouver, back to Victoria, on to Seattle, and finally back to Victoria (where it was refuelled and provisioned) all within twenty-four hours.

The *Princess Victoria* was remodelled in 1930 to make space for fifty automobiles, but, as the Depression grew worse, there were fewer passengers and therefore a need for fewer ships. In 1934, the *Princess Victoria* was moored at Newcastle Island off Nanaimo, where it became a popularly priced hotel (five dollars got you a two-berth upper-deck room for a week plus use of the ship's galley). By 1937 the economy was improving, traffic was even heavier than it had been in 1929, and the *Princess Victoria* was back in service. Its last voyage was a return trip between Vancouver and Nanaimo on August 21, 1950. After being laid up for a time it went for scrap, and its hull was sold to the Tahsis Lumber Company for use as a fuel barge. On March 10, 1953, while under tow, it struck a rock ten miles north of Sechelt and sank in deep water.

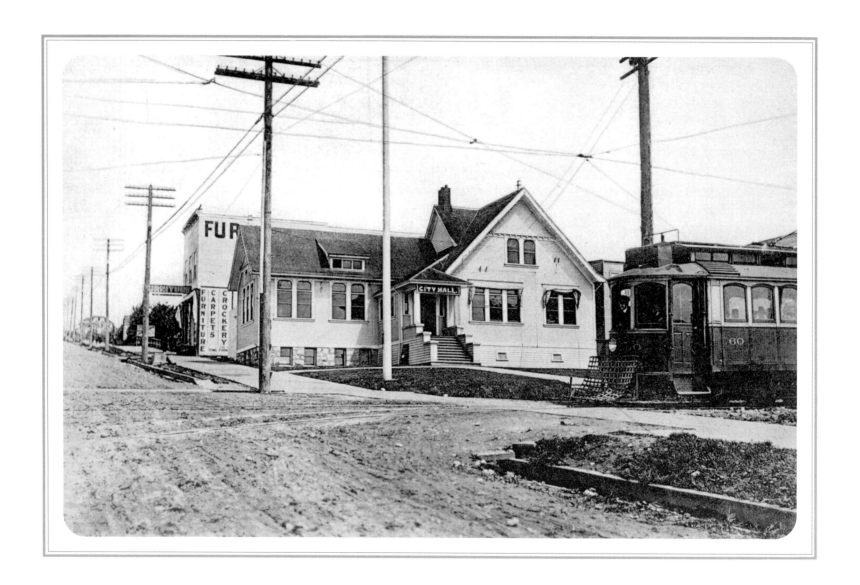

NORTH VANCOUVER CITY HALL

The Municipality of North Vancouver came into being in 1891 in response to the petition of twenty-two citizens. Strange as it might seem, the community's municipal office was located in the Inns of Court Building at Hastings and Hamilton in Vancouver. All council meetings, with the exception of one statutory meeting a year that had to be held in North Vancouver, were held there.

By 1903 the council voted to build a municipal hall. Three lots on the northeast corner of First and Lonsdale were purchased for $500 from Alfred St. George Hamersley. Hamersley, a wealthy English lawyer, had purchased the Arthur Heywood Lonsdale property (which included Moodyville) in 1905. Lonsdale, a London financier, held the mortgage on Sewell Moody's Burrard Inlet Lumber Mills and had foreclosed on it in the 1880s. Hamersley's North Vancouver Land and Improvement Company subdivided the Lower Lonsdale area, and this attracted a number of settlers.

The new municipal hall, a reflection of current domestic architectural taste, cost something less than $6,000 and was designed to permit later additions. To help meet the cost of the new building, all council members donated their allowances for 1903 – a gift, in total, of $3,600. The building pictured was opened in the fall of 1904. Above the door can be seen the words "City Hall." By 1907, the developing centre of the municipality felt that its interests were too divergent from those of the loggers and farmers of Lynn Valley and Capilano Canyon, and so North Vancouver opted for city status. On May 13, 1907, the City of North Vancouver came into existence, and the municipal hall became the city hall. Only five years later the city sold the building for $93,650 (a price that reflected boom-time real estate prices) to the federal government, which wanted it for a post office.

In 1912, North Vancouver was very much a city of dreams. Local publications speculated on the CPR building around the head of Burrard Inlet to their city and a second company constructing a scenic incline railway to the top of Grouse Mountain. Neither project ever came to be. Then there was the PGE Railway being built from North Vancouver to Fort George. Begun in 1913, it wasn't finished until 1956! The papers of the day also talked of a traffic and rail bridge over the Second Narrows as though it were an accomplished fact (it wasn't opened until 1925). It was also announced in 1912 that there was a plan afoot that could result in the building of a road and rail tunnel under the First Narrows within two years. And then there was Grand Boulevard, the creation of the Mahon brothers, touted in the 1912 *Vancouver Annual* as "several miles in length – this magnificent residential thoroughfare ... is ... the longest and widest in the world."

The depression of 1913 hit North Vancouver hard, and dreams turned to nightmares. By 1933, 75 per cent of city property owners had lost their land for taxes, and both the city and municipality were in receivership. Recovery and the long dreamed of growth did, of course, come to North Vancouver, but not until after the Second World War.

Main And Hastings

For a number of reasons, Main and Hastings enjoyed a long history as an important Vancouver corner. First, before Granville Street became "Theatre Row" in the mid-1920s, most of the city's popular theatres were within a few-block radius of this corner. While it's true that the CPR's Opera House was on Granville near Georgia, popular vaudeville theatres and playhouses like the Avenue, Empress, Majestic, Royal, and Pantages were all near Main and Hastings. Even the early motion-picture theatres were close at hand; the Crystal, Bijou, National, and Edison, which opened in 1902 as Canada's first movie house, were only a short walk away.

The second (and more lasting) reason for the corner's importance is that, for half a century, it was the site of the city's public library. Andrew Carnegie had already donated four million dollars to assist library construction in the United States and Scotland when he was asked to fund a permanent library building in Vancouver. He wrote on March 6, 1901, offering $50,000 towards a free lending-library building, provided city council donate a site and agree to spend $5,000 a year on the library. The terms were accepted and the location was decided by referendum, with 746 for the Main and Hastings site and 407 against. It was the last time eastside residents outvoted their more affluent westside cousins; future public buildings like the post office, court house, customs house, and even the immigration building were all built west of Granville Street.

The library building, only partially visible on the left of the picture, was designed by G.W. Grant in what the city deemed a suitably monumental style. It was built of Gabriola Island sandstone at a cost of $40,200. The cornerstone was laid with due ceremony by the Masonic Grand Lodge of British Columbia on March 29, 1902, and the library opened in 1903. Eventually, the city's museum occupied the top floor. In 1957, the library moved to a new building on Burrard Street, and, in 1968, the museum relocated to the new Centennial Museum in Vanier Park. The building at Main and Hastings was renovated and put to other uses. The restored building is currently home to the Carnegie Centre, the downtown eastside's community centre.

More prominently featured in the postcard is the building across the street from the old library. It was designed and built for G.W. Dawson by Bedford Davidson in 1911. While its style is strictly commercial, the eight-storey building's clean lines and simple form make it appealing. It originally contained 125 offices. Now known as the Ford Building, it has been successfully converted to residential apartments.

There are often interesting little surprises in postcards. In the top right corner of the picture, note the feet and legs of someone whom we can only suppose to be a BC Electric lineman.

St. Paul's Hospital

An article in the 1912 *Vancouver Annual* (a promotional magazine published by the city's Progress Club, a forerunner of the Vancouver Board of Trade), after proclaiming that Vancouver's death rate was only 9.7 per 1,000, went on to say that "the lower mainland's beautiful climate must be recognized when these figures are compared with the death rates of other parts of the world." Did the Progress Club really believe we owed it all to climate?

The climate may, indeed, have been salutary, but other factors helped give Vancouver a relatively low death rate. The comparative youthfulness of the population, the lack of extreme poverty, the early presence of a public health officer who had real power to act, and the 1887 city health by-law, under which medical and nursing care were provided to the poor without charge, were all important contributing factors. First-class hospitals also did their part in keeping Vancouverites out of the cemetery.

One of these fine hospitals was St. Paul's, which opened its doors on November 24, 1894, and wasn't long in establishing an enviable reputation. It was founded and staffed by the Roman Catholic Sisters of Charity of Providence, a French-Canadian order whose mother house was in Montreal. The Sisters of Charity had already established St. Mary's Hospital in New Westminster in 1886. The original St. Paul's was a frame building consisting of three storeys and an attic. When it was built its location was considered remote, being literally at the end of the Burrard Street trail.

In less than twenty years, the building was found to be inadequate to the growing needs of the city, and the construction of a new hospital was soon under way. Designed by Robert F. Tegen, and built by the Norton Griffith Steel Construction Company, the new St. Paul's Hospital was made of reinforced concrete. It was faced with Devny Penton Paving Brick and terracotta trim, while a red tile roof completed the Italian Renaissance effect. One of the special features of the building was the terracotta cross, which was "illuminated by electricity at night."

The new building incorporated the latest technology of the day, having its own emergency power plant, a built-in vacuum cleaning system, and oil-fired furnaces. As well, according to the *Vancouver Daily Province,* there was an "inter-communicating telephone system ... arranged so that the executive staff [could] communicate with one another in any part of the house ... [and] a silent electric call system for calling nurses ... doing away with the annoying ringing of bells, a constant worry to patients so often heard in hospitals." There were three large operating rooms that were up-to-date in every way, and on the roof, three spacious solariums. The chapel had a seating capacity of 150, which was the number of patients the hospital could accommodate. The new hospital was officially opened, with appropriate ceremony, on December 8, 1913 – the Feast of the Immaculate Conception.

THE BC ELECTRIC'S SECOND STATION

On August 6, 1912, the first interurban pulled into the BC Electric's new building in downtown Vancouver. At about the same time, some 300 office employees moved into the company's new head offices. The elegant five-storey structure housed both the corporate offices and the interurban depot. It was a vast improvement over the old two-storey building that had opened on the same site on 1898.

This second station, on the southwest corner of Hastings and Carrall, was designed by Sumervell and Putnam, an architectural firm noted for its finely detailed designs. Perhaps the firm's best-known building was the elegant Birks Building at Georgia and Granville, which was completed in November 1913. Construction of the $420,000 BC Electric Building began in the summer of 1911. It had a 190-foot frontage on Carrall and a 71-foot frontage on Hastings; it was of reinforced concrete, faced with brick veneer and terracotta trim. Unfortunately, grit and grime soon dulled the detailing that gave the building its special appeal. Two tracks ran through it, providing cover on the all too frequent days when Vancouver offered something other than endless sunshine.

An early morning rain probably ended just before our picture was taken. While it cannot be said with absolute certainty, the tram about to depart appears to be No. 1400, a combined passenger and express car built by the American Car Company in 1910. This car, like others ordered at the same time, featured such luxuries as rattan seats with headrests, two toilets, and a water cooler. Fifty-five feet and four inches long, it was one of the company's more powerful cars and could be run in multiple-unit trains.

It is interesting that even though "tram" was the popular British name for a passenger car on a street railway, in Vancouver and the Lower Mainland a tram was an interurban, *never* a streetcar. Possibly the local usage arose out of the fact that the original Vancouver-New Westminster interurban line, which opened in 1891, was owned and operated by the Westminster and Vancouver Tramway Company before it was taken over by the BC Electric.

Like many buildings in Vancouver, the BC Electric's combined head office and station served its original purpose for only a relatively short time – forty-two years. The last interurban to leave Carrall Street departed for the car barn in New Westminster at 1:30 AM on July 15, 1954. The waiting room through which fifty million people had passed was closed, trolley wires were taken down, and tracks were torn up. Diesel buses and trolley coaches were the order of the day. The BC Electric – government-owned BC Hydro as of August 1, 1961 – having constructed a magnificent new office building on Helmcken between Hornby and Burrard, sold the old buildings to a U.S.-based development company for $700,000.

THE HOLLOW TREE

The peninsula separating Burrard Inlet from English Bay became Stanley Park in September 1888. Almost immediately, work began on the construction of a perimeter road. The vehicles at the time were, of course, all horse-drawn, so nothing much more than a dirt road was needed. It wasn't long, however, before traffic was such that some kind of surfacing became necessary.

Because there wasn't any gravel close by, calcified seashells were used for the roadbed. These shells came from the Native midden at Whoi-Whoi, a village near what is now Lumberman's Arch. They covered a hectare to a depth of two and a half metres, and enough were dug up to surface the whole of what had come to be called the Park Road. While it seemed adequate at the time, the surface of seashells was soon broken down by the growing number of automobiles that were allowed into the park after 1905. By 1911, all eight and a half miles of road had been macadamized; that is, coated with a layer of small broken stones bound with asphalt.

A popular stopping point for tourists was the Hollow Tree, between Prospect and Ferguson Points. The Parks Board sold the photographic concession to the highest bidder. Not very many people owned cameras, and having the exclusive right to sell commercial photographs of visitors posing in the tree made for a lucrative business. While the commercial photographers have long since gone, tourists still stop by to have their pictures taken in front of what remains of Stanley Park's Hollow Tree.

SIWASH ROCK

Stanley Park's Siwash Rock gained fame when the Native myth associated with it was retold in 1911 by Pauline Johnson in her *Legends of Vancouver*. As she tells it, the story began long ago when a young chief brought home a northern woman to be his bride. In time, a child was expected. On the day when the birth was to take place, the couple went swimming according to the custom of their people. Tradition demanded that before the child was born its parents had to be so clean that no wild animal could pick up their scent. Presently, the mother-to-be went ashore to have her child, and her husband plunged back into the water, knowing that if his child was to be pure, he must be spotless.

As the chief swam, four giant men approached in a canoe. They ordered him out of the way, but he remained directly in their course. Even though they were agents of Sagalie Tyee, the Deity, they could not touch him, for should they do so they would become mere humans. As they considered what to do, they heard the cry of a newborn child drifting across the water and realized why they had been defied.

It was then that the one who steered the canoe spoke to the swimmer. He told the young chief that because he had been brave and defied them in order to capture the chance of a pure life for his child, he would never die but, rather, would stand as a monument to paternal purity. As the young man's foot touched the shore, he was transformed into a pillar of rock, now known as Siwash Rock. And nearby, in the forest, can be found a large rock with a small one beside it – the shy bride and her baby.

THE CITY HALL ON WESTMINSTER AVENUE

The towered and turreted building between Hastings and Pender on Westminster Avenue (later Main Street) started its life as the city market and ended it as an annex to the public library. From May 1898 until December 1928, it was Vancouver's city hall. The building was erected in 1889, designed by C.O. Wickenden (the architect of Christ Church Cathedral) and contracted by H.F. Keefer. Keefer had built the CPR line from Port Moody to Vancouver and, later, was the moving force in the company that gave the city its first water system. The structure was of red brick from the Bowen Island brickyard, in which David Oppenheimer, the city's mayor, had a large interest. Unfortunately, as it turned out, the brick was not of the highest quality, and the foreman, Dancing Jim McDonald, reported that the building showed signs of not being able to stand the strain of a second storey. The architect solved the problem by incorporating twin towers that acted as buttresses on either side of the half-completed building.

When the building opened the basement gave farmers, who entered from the lane, a space in which to sell horses, cows, pigs, and other large animals; the main floor provided space to sell poultry and small farm produce; the second floor housed an auditorium, with a stage and kitchen for making tea and coffee as well as "dainties for balls, banquets, etc."; and the tower provided space for the janitor. This tower later became the first home of the Vancouver City Archives.

In November 1896, city council decided to convert the market hall into a new city hall. At that point, the city offices were sharing an 1886 frame building on Powell Street with the police station and jail. Even though that structure had been enlarged to three times its original 2,000 square feet, it was still crowded and inadequate. On June 16, 1897, city council called for tenders to convert the market hall into a city hall. While we can presume that farmers protested the loss of their market hall, it nevertheless reopened as Vancouver City Hall in May 1898. The auditorium remained until 1910, when the second floor became an enlarged council chamber and offices.

The building served as city hall until January 1, 1929, when the municipalities of Point Grey and Vancouver South became part of the city of Vancouver. This amalgamation meant that more space was needed for civic offices. The much larger Holden Building on Hastings Street became the temporary city hall, and the old red-brick building became the reading room for the neighbouring public library.

At the end of 1931, the central tower was removed; in 1948, the cones that topped the turrets were removed. These distinguishing features had decayed to the point where they were considered unsafe. Apparently, "preventative maintenance" was not a priority in civic budgets of the 1930s and 1940s. Nor, it would seem, was heritage preservation a popular concern in the 1950s, for there was no protest when the building was torn down in 1958.

The 300-Block West Pender Street

West Pender Street, between Abbot and Granville, never became established as a prestigious business address. East of Abbott, Pender was Chinatown's main thoroughfare, with storefronts wearing the exotic countenance of the Orient. West of Granville, in the years before the First World War, Pender was still residential and considered to be part of the West End. The piece in the middle, however, seemed to lack identity and personality. Pender Street's apparent lack of significance probably related to the fact that a city can only have so many "main streets," and it was the streets blessed with streetcar tracks that attracted commercial growth. Streetcars ran along both Hastings and Cordova, one and two blocks north of Pender, respectively. How could Pender compete?

Despite its lack of star billing, Pender does have one block – the stretch between Hamilton and Homer – that has gained some distinction, if only because time has passed it by. The block looks much as it did in 1910. While nearly all the buildings are vintage structures, two deserve special mention. On the south side of the street stands an architectural gem, a small "temple bank" in Beaux-Arts, Neo-Classical style, designed by Hooper and Watkinson in 1907 for the BC Permanent Loan Company. The building retains some of the city's finest Tiffany-style stained glass as well as outstanding architectural detailing. The decorative castings were the work of Fraser and Garrow, who advertised themselves as being "perfectly at home in any manner of work that makes for the embellishment of interiors or exteriors."

On the north side of the street, the most interesting building is a colourful brick structure with stone banding. In 1910 its upper floors were occupied by the Dominion Hall and the Erisman Dancing Academy. In the basement was Vancouver's first commercial bowling alley, the Pender Street Bowling Alley, which advertised "8 continuous Up-to-Date Alleys; 4 Alleys Reserved for Ladies." On the ground floor was the Canada Cycle and Motor (CCM) Company, selling 2–, 4–, and 7– (yes 7–) cylinder Russell automobiles. Bicycles sold included the Cleveland, Perfect, Brantford, Massey-Harris, Imperial, Rambler, and Blue Flyer. In the 1920s and 1930s the company's own CCM bicycles became the most popular in Canada.

Probably the building is best remembered as the home of various shipbuilding and waterfront unions from the mid-1940s to the late 1960s. Upstairs were offices and the Boilermakers Hall, later known as the Pender Auditorium. In the basement was the Boilermakers Bowling Alley. Vancouver's very own Communist bookstore, the Peoples' Co-op Book Store, was at street level. At the time it was one of the city's best bookshops.

To see what Vancouver looked liked in 1910, just walk along the 300-block West Pender. It is to be hoped that this significant cityscape will not only be preserved but, eventually, will be restored to its original appearance.

"Automobiling" In Vancouver

A September 24, 1899, news item in the *Daily News-Advertiser* read: "The first automobile ever seen in British Columbia moved gently but swiftly over the paved streets of Vancouver today, with W.H. Armstrong at the crank. It is run by steam. The beautiful horseless carriage answered the steering gear to a hair's breadth as with rubber tires it is noiselessly rolled along the asphalt with a motive power entirely hidden from view. The car in appearance is very similar to a small buggy ... and carries a small bell to warn people of its approach."

William Armstrong was an engineer and senior partner in Armstrong, Morrison and Company, a successful firm that specialized in heavy construction. Armstrong doubtless selected his automobile with care. He had both the knowledge to choose wisely and the money to buy the best. He bought a Stanley Steamer that cost $650 in Newton, Massachusetts, where it was manufactured, and another $350 to get it to Vancouver. His choice of vehicle was logical in 1899, when over two-thirds of the cars made in the United States were either steam-powered or electric-powered. It wasn't until after the First World War that the internal combustion engine finally had the field all to itself.

Vancouver's first automobile dealership was that of Ernest and Walter Stark. In 1901 they became the agents for Oldsmobile, the first car to be mass produced on the assembly line. Oldsmobile was also the first company to develop a network of dealerships and to advertise widely. Ads of the day claimed that it was cheaper to run a car than it was to keep a horse and buggy. At $650, the Oldsmobile was priced to be attractive to the middle class.

It took time for automobiles to be seen as anything more than luxuries for those who enjoyed "automobiling" as a kind of sport. By 1904, however, the provincial government felt it necessary to pass "An Act to Regulate the Speed and Operation of Motor Vehicles on Highways." For the first time motor vehicles had to be registered with the superintendent of the provincial police in Victoria. Once registered, a permit and licence would be issued to the owner upon payment of a two-dollar fee. In 1904, only thirty-two motor vehicle licences were issued, and by 1907 there were still only 275 automobiles in BC.

It was on July 23, 1907, that seven car owners agreed to form an automobile club. They called a meeting for July 31 at the O'Brien Hall on Homer Street, where twenty car owners brought the Vancouver Automobile Club into being. Its first official club rally was held on Labour Day, 1907, and consisted of a run around Stanley Park. Eleven cars started out, but only five made it all the way around the park. Pictured at Prospect Point are some of these early motoring enthusiasts. Interestingly, four, if not all five, of the vehicles are Oldsmobiles (the fifth – the one with the roof – may be a Rambler, though it, too, looks suspiciously like an Olds).

GLENCOE LODGE: THE PERSONAL TOUCH

Glencoe Lodge was the creation of Jean Mollison, a Scotswoman who immigrated to Canada in May 1888 to join her older sister, who had come out a year before armed with a letter of introduction to Lord Strathcona, president of the CPR. Her sister was made the first manager of the Banff Springs Hotel, and when Jean arrived she became her assistant housekeeper. From there, Jean went on to manage the railway's Fraser Canyon Hotel at North Bend and then the Chateau Lake Louise in Banff National Park.

In April 1906, B.T. Rogers, president of the BC Sugar Refinery and a director of the CPR, bought two houses that the railroad had built on the northwest corner of Georgia and Burrard. He raised the buildings, built two storeys under them, and joined them together, thus creating a residential hotel at a cost of $30,000. He then asked Miss Mollison to lease and manage it. She declined at first, but, when Rogers offered her three months' free rent, and one of his fellow CPR directors offered her $20,000 to furnish the hotel as she wished, she accepted. There was always speculation that this scenario unfolded at the suggestion of Lord Strathcona himself. At any rate, under Miss Mollison's management, Glencoe Lodge immediately became Vancouver's most exclusive hotel.

By the time the hotel was enlarged in 1912, it had become the preserve of the city's self-anointed elite and of visitors who required something better than the nearby Hotel Vancouver's best. The guest list included celebrities like Sir Wilfred Laurier, MacKenzie King, Lord and Lady Aberdeen, and Ellen Terry. The Glencoe also had a number of permanent guests – people like the stockbroker C.M. Oliver and Mrs. Oliver. Furthermore, the Glencoe Lodge was home to the Canadian Women's Club, the American Women's Club, and the Vancouver Philharmonic Society.

Miss Mollison's personal touch was evident in everything about the hotel. The drawing room reflected her eclectic tastes: tables from British India; a desk, chair, and jardinière from China; and William Morris's "Liberty" print wallpaper lived together in a happy and fashionable mix. Glencoe Lodge was advertised as "a thoroughly comfortable and splendidly furnished hotel" and as "ideal and much favoured by ladies travelling without escort."

Glencoe Lodge lasted until 1932, when the Depression forced Miss Mollison to close. Some of her permanent guests owed her a total of over $11,000, which she was never able to collect. She accepted her predicament philosophically, saying, in her finest Scottish brogue, "You canna' tak' the breeks aff a Hielanman." After the hotel building was razed in 1935 the property was leased to Standard Oil as a gas station and parking lot site for $225 a month. Almost thirty-five years later, construction started on the towers of the Royal Centre, which now occupies the property.

NEW WESTMINSTER CITY MARKET

The first of New Westminster's city markets opened November 4, 1892. The building stood on Lytton Square, below Church Street, and was essentially a long shed backing onto the waterfront. The market was intended to serve a wide area, and the reeves of Delta, Surrey, Langley, Maple Ridge, and Chilliwack were present for its opening.

Getting to market in the 1890s wasn't all that easy for those who lived any distance away. They could travel either by sternwheeler on the river or by horse and buggy along the very poor country roads. Even when those travelling by road got to the "highway," the Yale Road, conditions weren't much better. Those who had to cross the Fraser River to get to New Westminster paid ten cents each and boarded the *Surrey*, the new ferry that was put into service in 1891.

The first market survived less than six years before disaster struck. On the night of September 10, 1898, three-quarters of New Westminster was burned to the ground. Since the fire had started in the Brakman and Ker wharf, which was immediately west of the market building, it was only a matter of minutes before the city market was on fire, too. Damage to the city was devastating; most of the commercial centre was wiped out, and virtually all federal and provincial offices were destroyed. Even the fire hall burned down!

At 1:30 PM on July 23, 1904, life changed for Fraser Valley travellers making their way to the Royal City: the bridge across the Fraser River was officially opened. Their lives changed further on October 3, 1910, when the BC Electric's Chilliwack interurban line – the longest in Canada – opened. The market building that was erected after the fire is the one pictured. To the left is the livery barn, where farmers stabled their horses for the day. Friday was market day in New Westminster, and, by 1911, the approximate date of the picture, many people travelled on a market-day "Special" interurban from points as far away as Chilliwack. While the trams were popular, the rows of buggies and democrats suggest that many still made their own way to market. The circle of men is gathered around T.J. Trapp, who is conducting a horse auction. Horses, cattle, feed, and even household effects were sold at the weekly auction.

By 1925 the Front Street site was no longer suitable for the market, as road traffic and railway tracks caused excessive congestion. A by-law asking for $60,000 for a new market was put to the voters in 1925, but they turned it down. Fate, however, played a hand in the proceedings, and the city market again burned to the ground. A new, three-storey market building opened on April 30, 1926, on Columbia Street, directly above the old market. In 1947 the market was again moved. This third building was sold to David Spencer Limited, who in turn sold it to Eaton's, who eventually sold it to the Army and Navy Department Store. The fourth market, built after the Second World War, was located farther west at 1051 Columbia Street. Its successor is the present-day market at New Westminster Quay, where the market tradition, started over a century ago by a city council with vision and foresight, still lives on in the Royal City.

VANCOUVER'S SILLIEST PICTURE?

It is wonderful what a little imagination on the part of a resourceful photographer can do. One of Vancouver's highly popular observation cars appears to be circling Stanley Park. At no time, though, did streetcar tracks run through the park. Not that enterprising individuals didn't have a go at trying to get streetcars into Stanley Park. The first attempt was in 1896, when the Consolidated Railway and Light Company requested civic permission and was turned down. In August 1903, city council was asked by some citizens to allow the carline to be extended from Georgia and Chilco to the athletic grounds at Brockton Point. While the idea may sound unattractive today, remember that most people making their way to Brockton Point in 1903 had to walk about a mile from the end of the carline. As it happened, the BC Electric had other priorities and didn't support the idea. In 1910, the Electric Railway Construction Company asked Parks Board permission to run an electric tramline around the park. Though some Parks Board members favoured the idea, nothing came of it.

Even though the BC Electric's observation cars never travelled through Stanley Park, they were always immensely popular. Built in the company's New Westminster shops in 1909, they were patterned after similar cars in Montreal. In fact, the BC Electric bought the plans from the Montreal Tramway Company for twenty-five cents! Car No. 123 was put into service in Victoria, Car No. 124 in Vancouver. A decade later it made more economic sense for both observation cars to be used in Vancouver, and Car No.123 was transferred to Vancouver.

A surprise feature of the two-hour, fifty-cent sight-seeing tour of Vancouver was the opportunity to buy a souvenir picture of the observation car with *you in it*. The "surprise" was managed with great efficiency. About a block from the Carrall Street station the car stopped, ostensibly to allow passengers time to admire the architectural features associated with the New Dodson Hotel. From the second-storey window of a room he had rented for the season, Harry Bullen took the picture and counted the number of families on the car in order to get some idea of how many of his photos he would sell. The observation car rolled on, and the photographer developed and printed the pictures. He then got on his bike and rode to Granville and Robson in time to deposit the photos in a box at the rear of the passing observation car, which by then was nearing the end of its journey. The conductor took the pictures from the box and sold them to the passengers. Meanwhile, Bullen peddled back to the hotel to be ready for the next trip.

The last trip took place on September 17, 1950. By then there were simply not enough miles of track left in the city to make a worthwhile sight-seeing trip possible. The BC Electric stored the cars, having offered them to the city, assuming that one or both could be displayed either at Kitsilano Beach or in Stanley Park. When the city showed no interest in the idea, the cars were scrapped in 1952.

KITSILANO BEACH

Kitsilano's popularity goes back a long way. It was originally called Greer's Beach after Sam Greer, the area's first settler. Even though he claimed to have bought the 160 acres bounded by First Avenue on the south, Trafalgar on the west, the First Nations village of Snauq on the east, and the waterfront on the north in 1892, Greer had no title. In 1894 the CPR, claiming the property as a part of its land grant, challenged his ownership. The railway was ultimately successful in securing its claim. Greer's house and barn were levelled, and on their site was built the first and succeeding bathhouses.

The first bathhouse was a primitive affair, combining a dance hall, bathhouse, and boathouse. It was privately owned and served a colony of campers that found Greer's Beach to be an attractive alternative to English Bay (which, by the 1890s, was both highly popular and overcrowded). It shouldn't be thought that these campers were early-day hippies. Quite the contrary. They were members of fashionable pioneer families who created a secluded and exclusive summer camp. Some families may have had as many as four tents: the first to be used as a bedroom, the second as a drawing-room, the third as a dining room, and the fourth for the Chinese help. They got to camp either by rowing across English Bay or by taking the streetcar to the closest stop (at Third and Granville) and walking the rest of the way.

Things changed in 1905, when the CPR decided to open the area for residential development. As early as 1886, the railway had announced plans to build a deep-sea terminal and railway yards on what is now Kits Point. A downturn in the economy in the 1890s, coupled with loud civic protest, convinced the CPR that it might be best to shelve these ideas, at least for a time. By 1905, it was apparent that the area contained prime residential property that could be sold at a substantial profit. It was suggested that the name for the new area should honour Chief Khahtsallanough of the local Native community. The name was, of course, simplified to "Kitsilano," which was much easier for English tongues to manage. Also in 1905, on July fourth, the streetcar line was extended to the foot of Vine Street. This meant that many more campers would now find their way to Kitsilano Beach. In fact, the number of campers became so high that, in 1908, the city had to ban camping. Sanitary conditions (or, more accurately, the lack thereof) made the tent city that sprang up every summer a health hazard.

Pictured is the Kitsilano Beach Bathhouse and Boathouse that replaced the original dance hall and bathhouse, which were torn down in 1904. The picture may date from 1909, the year in which a small group of local citizens bought four and three-quarter acres west of Yew Street from the CPR for $1,500 and turned it into a public waterfront park. In 1910, the city reimbursed these citizens and took over the management of what we now know as Kitsilano Beach.

THE FIRST AND THE LAST

In 1860 the first priest of the French Roman Catholic Oblates of Mary Immaculate, Father Leon Fouquet, arrived in New Westminster. He was soon instructed to find a suitable site for a mission and Indian boarding school somewhere along the Fraser River. On February 11, 1861, he chose a spot thirty-five miles upstream from the Royal City, the site of present-day Mission City. Fouquet expressed the hope that Native children would be freed from the primitive ways of camp life so that they might receive a basic education and be taught the Christian faith.

St. Mary's Mission and Residential School for Native boys opened in November 1863, with an enrolment of forty-two. It was the first permanent Native boarding school on the BC Mainland. The boys were taught religion, the three Rs, geography, carpentry, agriculture, and music. In November 1868, two sisters of the Order of St. Ann arrived to open a girls' convent at St. Mary's. The girls' academic program was augmented by housekeeping, sewing, gardening, and singing.

The planned transcontinental railroad meant that the mission and school would have to be moved to higher ground. The CPR's track was to follow the riverbank, passing right through the mission property. In 1882, the Oblates began the slow and difficult task of relocating to a new site half a mile north of the river. The land was so heavily forested that it took more than a decade to clear adequate space for buildings, playgrounds, and farmland.

The new residences provided accommodation for fifty boys and fifty girls. Connected with the boys' school was a large building containing a band room, carpenter and shoemaker shops, a blacksmith shop, a recreation hall, a woodshed, a root house, a tool house, stables, cattle sheds, a piggery, and a hen house. The laundry and the bakery were attached to the girls' school. The building pictured is the girls' dormitory, beyond which is the chapel. Children came to the school from as far away as Sechelt, Squamish, Lillooet, Douglas (at the head of Harrison Lake), and some Interior villages. By 1896 St. Mary's School had nearly sixty acres under cultivation. Both the boys' and girls' residences had vegetable, fruit, and flower gardens.

The last class graduated from the old St. Mary's Mission and Residential School in 1959. In 1961 a new grade school and residence was opened under the auspices of the federal Department of Indian Affairs. All the original buildings on St. Mary's Mission lands were demolished. The last of the Oblates and Sisters of St. Ann left in 1974, when the land and new buildings erected in the 1960s were purchased by the provincial government. In 1984 St. Mary's grade school and residence was phased out, its students being the last Native children to be integrated into the public school system. St. Mary's Mission and Residential School was not only the first residential school established on the Mainland, it was also the last boarding school for Native children to operate in British Columbia.

THE VANCOUVER CLUB

While the origins of the Vancouver Club are, to a degree, uncertain – early minutes have been lost – it seems that in the summer of 1889 a group of businessmen decided to form a club. In February 1890, they rented "a splendid set of rooms" in the Lefevre Block at Hastings and Seymour. For some unknown reason, the club lost its premises to W.J. Meaken in July of 1890. The members were "locked out" by Meaken, who was the proprietor of a restaurant and boarding house in the same building. After this false start, the club finally got going in late 1890, when land at the foot of Hornby Street was bought from the CPR for $12,500. On June 19, 1891, a member and well-known architect, C.O. Wickenden, was instructed to prepare drawings for a clubhouse. On July 24, plans for the building were approved and the architect called for tenders. Edward Cook was the contractor chosen, and he agreed to erect the building for $22,728. The building was first occupied in the spring of 1894.

The ground or basement level included space for a number of facilities, such as a bar room and a billiard room, the latter being "fitted up with both gas and electric light with the most improved designs of shades over the tables." Just off the billiard room the original design included a bowling alley. On the first floor was the reception hall, with "a noble stag's head" mounted over a massive fireplace. Beyond the reception hall was a writing room, a large reading room, and a wine room "fitted out with a refrigerator – exceedingly commodious – a good feature." The second floor provided space for two card rooms, the main dining room, and a private dining room. Off the main dining room was a wide balcony. The third floor initially provided bedrooms for help, for members who chose to live at the club, and for club guests.

By 1903 space was becoming a problem, and land was purchased to the west side of the existing clubhouse in order to make possible the building of a two-storey addition, which would accommodate an additional billiard room, ballroom, and enlarged dining room. Our picture shows the clubhouse after the addition was built. The bowling alley was torn out in 1905 to make room for servants quarters. To replace the bowling alley a bowling green was constructed on the grounds, and lawn bowls at ten cents a game was soon a popular feature of club life. Also outdoors was a squash court.

As the city grew, so did the number of men seeking membership in the Vancouver Club. In December 1910, it was proposed that a new clubhouse be built next door to the original building. This new clubhouse was ready for occupancy on January 1, 1914. The old building had been sold the previous year to J.D. Cobbald. After it had stood empty for a year, it was used from 1915 to 1918 as the headquarters for the 72nd Seaforth Highlanders of Canada. From 1919 to 1922 it was home to the Great War Veterans Association, and it served to house the Quadra Club from 1923 to 1930, when it was finally demolished. A very attractive mini-park now occupies the original site.

PUSHING BACK THE FRONTIER

Until the Russell Hotel opened on January 21, 1908, accommodation in New Westminster could only be described as frontier. Travellers who wanted anything other than the rough and ready had to stay in Vancouver. E.J. Fader, a New Westminster industrialist of considerable wealth, built the Russell in order to accommodate those with whom he would be doing business. Located at 740 Carnarvon Street, between Alexander and Begbie, the new hotel was directly across the street from Fader's home and, conveniently, on the streetcar line.

The Russell Hotel was designed, in the Beaux-Arts Neo-Classical style, by Dalton and Everleigh, Vancouver architects. Originally planned as two storeys, the finished building of brick and stone rose to three floors. It had a frontage of 132 feet and cost $60,000 to build. Fader claimed that, finished and furnished, the hotel had cost him over $100,000. It had eighty rooms, fourteen of which were en suite. The dining room could accommodate 150 and quickly became the preferred local site for banquets. Events like the May Day dinners, the 1908 Canadian Manufacturers' Association luncheon, and the 1912 Minto Cup presentation banquet were held at the Russell. In addition to the lobby, offices, and dining room, the ground floor housed a large billiard room and Pthree sample rooms for travelling salesmen. Off Begbie Street, on a lower level was another room mandatory in any full-service hotel. As can be seen in the picture, the bar was "so arranged as to be on a side street".

Fader sold the hotel in 1910 to G. Hankey and Company of Vernon. It was the firm's owner, G. Alers Hankey, who, in 1912, had the six-storey Arundel Mansions built on Begbie Street next to the Russell. Thornton and Davis, another team of Vancouver architects, designed the reinforced concrete and brick apartment block. While its rows of bay windows gave the building a rather old-fashioned Victorian look, they also provided the suites with lots of light and fresh air.

Both buildings still exist and are little altered insofar as outward appearances are concerned. The Russell is now the College Place Hotel, and its bar and disco make it a popular New Westminster night spot. The Arundel is still an apartment block. Just as the Russell's convenient location near the CPR and BC Electric stations contributed to its success, so the fact that the College Place Hotel is handy to the SkyTrain station contributes to its success.

THE NORTH VANCOUVER FERRIES

The first scheduled ferry service between downtown Vancouver and North Vancouver came into being in 1893, when the Union Steamship Company signed an agreement with North Vancouver to make six return trips a day across Burrard Inlet. North Vancouver paid $100 a month for the service. In the summer of 1899, Union Steamships informed the municipal council that it would discontinue the service, as it had been unprofitable for some time. With no other alternative, the municipality decided to build its own ferry at a cost of $12,000. The *North Vancouver*, as it was called, went into service in 1900, with a one-way ticket for a foot passenger costing five cents and a monthly pass costing two dollars. The ship had one particular limitation: it loaded from the side and had to be turned around at each docking so vehicles would be facing the right way for off-loading.

In 1903 the North Vancouver Ferry and Power Company purchased the ferry service. All was not public-spirited altruism, however. The company was controlled by A. St. George Hamersley, an aristocratic English lawyer who came to Vancouver from New Zealand in 1888 following the Maori Wars. Hoping to sell real estate on the North Shore, Hamersley needed prospective buyers to believe that a fast, frequent, reliable, and reasonably priced ferry service was a certainty. And so he announced a new ferry.

The *St. George* was launched in 1905 by Wallace's Shipyard in False Creek. It was double-ended, to facilitate the loading process and fast turnaround time. By 1908 Hamersley and his partners realized their ferry service would never make money, and they wanted to be rid of it. North Vancouver was again forced to take over the ferries and operate them as a public utility. Soon after taking over the system, the city fathers gave the ferries numbers instead of names, and the *St. George* became *North Vancouver Ferry No. 2*.

Demand for service grew to the point that, by 1911, North Vancouver needed to replace the antique and inadequate *North Vancouver Ferry No. 1*. Built by Wallace's Shipyard in North Vancouver, *North Vancouver Ferry No. 3* was launched on February 27, 1911. The new ferry is pictured in the Vancouver ferry slip, which was located at the foot of Columbia Street. The picture, circa 1912 or 1913, was taken from the deck of a steamer docked at the Grand Trunk Pacific (later CNR) wharf, which was at the foot of Main Street in Vancouver and immediately east of the ferry slip. The single-funneled ship alongside the Evans, Coleman and Evans wharf is the *Princess Beatrice,* the first CPR vessel to be built in British Columbia.

Ferry No. 3 was taken out of regular service in 1948, to be used only as a relief vessel when either of the newer ferries – *No. 4* and *No. 5* – required an overhaul. Finally, in June of 1952 it was sold and became a floating store and shipwright's workshop on the Fraser River. The ferry service itself ended on August 30, 1958. In the nearly forty years during which an accurate tally was kept, the North Vancouver ferries carried 112,466,693 passengers. Not a bad record of service.

NEW WESTMINSTER'S ANNUAL FAIR

Two separate paths of destiny had to converge before New Westminster's annual fair at Queen's Park could become a reality. The first path led to the creation of the park in which a fair could be held. Queen's Park came into being at the behest of Colonel Richard Moody of the Royal Engineers. He was a man ahead of his time when he wrote the following to Governor Douglas on March 17, 1859: "Without the least sentimentality I grieve and mourn the destruction of these most glorious trees. What a grand old park the whole hill would make! I am reserving a very beautiful glen and adjoining land for the People's Park. I have already named it 'Queen's Ravine,' and trust you will approve. It divides the town (New Westminster) from the Military Reserve (Sapperton)." Queen's Ravine quickly became Queen's Park, and by 1886 enough land had been cleared for a racetrack and some additional open space. In 1888 the provincial government confirmed that Queen's Park had for all time been "reserved and set apart for the recreation and enjoyment of the public." The second path to the Royal City's annual fair was that blazed by the New Westminster District Agricultural Society, founded in December of 1867. The society held "annual events, awarding prizes for superior livestock and produce." By 1886 the society's performance warranted official recognition, and the organization became the Royal Agricultural and Industrial Society of British Columbia.

The convergence came in 1889, when construction of the first exhibition building was begun in Queen's Park. The Agricultural Building was ready for the 1890 exhibition. It was two stories high, of cruciform shape, and able to provide 15,000 square feet of display space. It appears on the left of the picture and was designed by George W. Grant, a prominent local architect. It wasn't long before the Manufacturers' Building (shown on the right of the picture), a Women's Christian Building (complete with a Women's Temperance Union Ladies' Rest Room on the upper floor), a large machinery annex, sheds and stables for livestock, and an ice rink were built. In front of the buildings pictured was a race track. In the words of the *Vancouver Daily World* of December 31, 1889, it was "as fine a race track as there is to be found in the Province, half a mile in length and 66 feet wide. The track (enclosing a ten acre athletic ground,) a beautifully levelled stretch." A grandstand was erected at the west end of the track.

All went reasonably well until 1929, when, early on the morning of July 14, virtually every building burned to the ground. Winston Churchill had already been invited to open the exhibition scheduled for September. The rubble was cleared, tents were erected to replace the lost buildings, and Churchill opened New Westminster's fair on time. Over 37,000 came to the Royal City's last major exhibition. The buildings were not rebuilt, and New Westminster's annual fair at Queen's Park passed into history.

STANLEY PARK PAVILION

Tyrolean *Gasthof* in a Vancouver city park? Sound unlikely? Believe it or not, that's exactly what Stanley Park's Refreshment Pavilion was intended to be! Of the six designs submitted to the Parks Board by Vancouver architects in 1910, the plan proposed by Otto W. Moberg was the one accepted. Moberg had come to Vancouver from his native Austria, and it was perfectly reasonable that his pavilion would be in an alpine style reminiscent of his homeland. While his design originally called for a log building, on January 25, 1911, the Parks Board told him to rework the plan using cut stone rather than logs. The contractor charged with building Moberg's Tyrolean inn was H.G. Patterson. Interestingly, Patterson's contract required that all subtrades were to be paid at union rates. Not that this clause ensured peace and harmony: on June 14, 1911, he had to ask for a three-month extension "in consequence of the work being held up by a strike."

The new Stanley Park Refreshment Pavilion represented two things: the Parks Board's will to upgrade facilities and its determination to manage park refreshment facilities internally rather than to lease them out as concessions, as had hitherto been the case. Even though the Pavilion was completed in 1912, it did not open until 1913, by which time the lease of the firm that operated existing park and beach food concessions had expired.

Regardless of what at first might seem to be an inappropriate style for an urban park on Canada's West Coast, the Pavilion was, and is, an eminently successful building, matched beautifully to its site. Costing $15,000 to build, it was described in the *Vancouver Daily Province* as being "of bungalow style with long sweeping verandas and balconies in the rough timber style" – a very English description of a very Austrian design! The main refreshment room was on the ground floor, "with soda water fountain and all the requisites of picnickers behind the counters." There was a second dining room on the upper floor. Furnishings cost $4,260.49 and included not only the "first-class soda fountain," but also tables and chairs for both dining rooms and verandas, a cash register, and a gramophone. The gramophone must have been a quality item, for it cost $180 – no small amount at that time.

The Pavilion was officially opened on May 7, 1913, when the Parks Board Commissioners tendered a banquet to civic representatives and other dignitaries. Mayor T.S. Baxter had the honour of officially opening the city's first municipally owned refreshment building. The building was immediately popular. To everyone's surprise, and doubtless to everyone's relief, it managed to show a profit in its very first year of operation. This it did even though, as a matter of policy, it was open year round, regardless of the weather. While the Pavilion is no longer the scene of elaborate dining and dancing, it has remained a popular Stanley Park landmark.

Interior Catholic Cathedral, Vancouver, B. C.

HOLY ROSARY CATHEDRAL

While many Quebec villages boast a grander church than Holy Rosary, its erection was a triumph for Vancouver's limited Roman Catholic population at the turn of the century. Their first church had been a modest frame structure built in 1889. Within a decade it was obvious that this building was inadequate and would have to be replaced. However, the parish was already $15,000 in debt and, furthermore, Roman Catholics made up only 11 per cent of the city's population. This meant there were 3,500 Roman Catholics, comprising about 800 families. The pastor, Father James McGuckin, was an Oblate of Irish birth and the first non-French-speaking priest of his order sent to British Columbia. When he suggested building a stone church in the French Gothic style, his parishioners must have wondered what had hit them! The Oblates of Mary Immaculate, who mortgaged their headquarters in France to pay for the new church, must also have been a little apprehensive about "McGuckin's Folly."

Nevertheless, plans went ahead and an architect, Thomas Ennor Julian, was hired. Julian had opened a practice in Vancouver in 1893 and had a less than distinguished career in spite of Holy Rosary, his only memorable creation. The builder was R.P. Foreshaw and Company, and the cornerstone for the new Parish Church of Our Lady of the Holy Rosary was laid on July 16, 1899. Even though Dunsmuir and Richards was not prime real estate when the church was built, the location and building do credit to the courage and vision of Father McGuckin and his relatively small congregation. Both the site and building turned out to be well-suited to the need of a future cathedral.

The church, which became the cathedral for the Archdiocese of Vancouver in 1916, has been popularly described as evocative of Chartes. While this may be stretching credulity, the design *is* successful. Holy Rosary's exterior of Galiano Island sandstone, asymmetrical towers and spires, transepts and rounded apse fulfil the popular image of what a church should look like. Today it remains a sophisticated version of the picture-book church building many children would recognize.

Harsh present-day critics find all sorts of design shortcomings in Holy Rosary. They tell us that the front elevation is too high for its width, the rose window is too crowded, the spires rise too abruptly from the towers, and so forth, and so on. But when it is the only "early French Gothic" cathedral in town, who cares! Through the years the interior has undergone a number of renovations; fortunately, they have been largely cosmetic. Now that massive sports arenas, office towers, and shopping complexes encroach on the downtown area, Vancouver is fortunate to have Holy Rosary Cathedral. It continues to provide an island of calm not only for those who pass through its portals, but also for those who simply pass by.

THE CPR'S THIRD STATION

In the years immediately before the First World War, the CPR seemed to be on a spending spree in Vancouver. A new sumptuous Hotel Vancouver was under construction, a pier that could accommodate the company's coastal fleet and ocean liners was being built, eight new *Princesses* were in service or under construction, and two new trans-Pacific *Empresses* were put in service. In addition, on June 19, 1907, a million-dollar train station, CPR's third since the railway first reached Vancouver in 1887, was announced. While the "old" station had been in use for less than a decade, its layout was such that it couldn't be efficiently enlarged. The need for more space could only be met by erecting a totally new facility. Designed by the Montreal firm of Barrott, Blackader and Webster, the new building was architecturally a distant cousin of New York's Pennsylvania Station, which, in turn, had been modelled after the Baths of Caracalla in Rome. Somehow, the grandeur that was ancient Rome was deemed to be an appropriate style for North American railway stations! Work started on the new station on May 31, 1912.

As our postcard (made from the architect's sketch) clearly suggests, a colonnade of pillars gave an impressive appearance to the 380-foot brick and stone Cordova Street building. The station was five storeys high on the street side and seven storeys high on the lower (or track) side. Beyond the large general waiting room, suitably featuring Roman arches and a coffered ceiling, were ticket offices, a baggage check room, news stand, ladies' waiting room, men's smoking room, and a typical CPR dining room – elegant and expensive.

The general waiting room was decorated with a series of paintings by Adelaide Langford, which, unfortunately, were so high that it was nearly impossible to see them, let alone appreciate them. Much more likely to catch the traveller's attention were what stood in the middle of the vast reception area – the marvellous glass-cased builders' models of the company's elegant steamships.

At track level, immigrant rooms – a special waiting room, lunch room, and bathroom – were provided for those emigrating from Asia. Also on the lower level were baggage, express, and supply rooms. As they made their way to one or other of the four tracks, walking along the 1,000-foot covered platforms to board the train, most passengers were totally unaware of the existence of these "below-stairs" facilities.

Had war not been declared on August 4, 1914, doubtless the CPR's impressive new train station and pier would have been opened with great celebration. However, people didn't feel much like a party in August 1914. While the pier has long since gone, the station remains as the SeaBus/SkyTrain station. It is a landmark recalling the glamour and excitement of train travel in the days of the CPR's *Imperial Limited.*

THE SUN TOWER

Vancouver's flamboyant and controversial mayor, L.D. Taylor, built the seventeen-storey Tower Building in 1911-12. Its chief tenant was to be his newspaper, the *Vancouver World*. Designed by W.T. Whiteway, it was erected at the corner of Beatty and Pender and was popularly known as the World Building. Taylor saw to it that his building was tall enough to take the title "tallest building in the Empire" away from the nearby Dominion Trust Building.

When the Tower Building was built, it was off the beaten track and had difficulty attracting tenants. By 1915 Taylor's financial situation was such that his newspaper had to move out, and by 1924, faced with bankruptcy, he had to sell the building to Bekins Moving and Storage Company. The *World,* together with another paper, the *Daily News-Advertiser,* was absorbed by the *Vancouver Sun*. The *Sun* was owned by Foley, Stewart, and Welsh, railway contractors who felt the need for a strong Liberal paper that would reflect their politics and defend their interests against the dominant paper of the day, the Conservative *Vancouver Daily Province.*

Through fate, the *Vancouver Sun* came to own and occupy the Tower Building. In early 1937 a fire destroyed the *Sun's* premises across the street at 125 West Pender. In need of a home, the paper bought the Tower Building, which then became the Sun Tower. Even though the newspaper moved out in 1964, the name has stuck. Although the Sun Tower is no longer the landmark it once was – modern high-rises have placed it in the shadows – its distinctive profile marks it as unique.

Five Mail Deliveries A Day

When can we look forward to five mail deliveries a day? Doubtless never! But we can look *back* to 1911, when there *were* five daily mail deliveries throughout the business district. There were also four deliveries in the "semi-business" section, three farther out, and even two home deliveries per day in the outlying residential districts.

It was in 1895 that Vancouver's post office was "raised to the dignity of a city office." In the same year the first mailboxes were installed, and four carriers were hired to initiate limited street delivery. It wasn't very long before the original post office at Pender and Granville was inadequate. A $500,000 contract was let in August 1905 for a new post office at Granville and Hastings, a location that wasn't universally appreciated. People on the east side felt the building should have been located in their part of town. While the CPR may have influenced the choice of site, the fact that it was within a stone's throw of both the railway station and boat docks was quite logical, as all mail entering or leaving the city had to be carried by train or ship.

Designed by the Department of Public Works, the post office was the first major public building in the city to be constructed of steel and reinforced concrete. It was architecturally very much of its day, with both Classical and Baroque detailing living happily together in the best Beaux-Arts Neo-Classical tradition. When it opened in February 1910, the new Vancouver Post Office had more floor space than any other post office in Canada. Replaced in 1958 by the new general post office on Georgia Street, the building is now part of the Sinclair Centre.

Vancouver's YWCA

The Vancouver branch of the YWCA grew out of the concern of a group of women at St. Andrew's Presbyterian Church. Their particular anxiety related to the presence of a number of young women who had found their way to the city, "eager for work and adventure," in the early 1890s. Many found neither, and the women of St. Andrew's formed a committee to see what could be done for friendless young girls away from home.

Initially, the women opened a room for the girls at 633 Homer, not far from St. Andrew's. Today the "room" would probably be called a drop-in centre. It quickly became apparent that more organization was needed, and in 1896 the group affiliated with the Dominion Council of the YWCA. The first president was Mrs. Robert Skinner, and the first general secretary was a Miss Cumming.

For its first centre, the Vancouver YWCA rented a house at Pender and Richards. By 1900 the YWCA was able to buy a building of its own, and it moved to 591 Howe Street. When it was rumoured that a livery stable was about to become a new neighbour, the YWCA exchanged the house for the vacant property on the northeast corner of Burrard and Dunsmuir, where the building pictured was erected in 1905-06. It had a residential quality about it, not only to give it a "home-away-from-home" look, but also to enable it to blend in with the surrounding houses. Until after the First World War, Burrard was still very much a residential street. The new building was opened in 1906 by the lieutenant-governor, the Honourable James Dunsmuir.

It was only three years before the building needed to be enlarged, and in 1910 a matching wing added to the east doubled its size. The enlarged residence could accommodate fifty-two women, and it contained a dining room, sitting room, sewing room, and laundry, all of which were available to guests. In 1924 a modern gymnasium was added to the building.

A typical year in the life of the YWCA would have been 1911, when the special secretary for the Travellers Aid Program met 709 trains and 521 boats. Some 2,074 travellers were provided with temporary accommodation, and 2,218 women were assisted in various ways at railway stations and wharves. In the same year the YWCA found positions for 1,064 women, and its immigration bureau received and placed fourteen parties of women sent to Canada by the British Women's Emigration Association. While the YWCA offered a number of classes, the one described as being the most practical and useful focused on "household training." Most of the young women who found employment did so either as domestics or as chars, or as kitchen help in homes and institutions. Vancouver owes much to the vision and active concern of the women of St. Andrew's Presbyterian Church, whose courage brought into being the local YWCA, which still meets the special needs of women in what is now a large and not always friendly city.

"PROGRESS"

In 1910 Vancouverites pointed to Granville Street with pride. After all, it bore all the signs of progress and the success they so avidly sought. At the foot of the street was the CPR's handsome eight-storey station, a building, they could say, that was already slated for replacement by a bigger and finer terminus. The clock tower of the about-to-be-opened post office at Granville and Hastings overshadowed its 1892 stone predecessor on the southwest corner of Pender and Granville as local pundits boasted that their new post office had the most floor space of any post office in Canada.

While later generations would find the power poles and overhead wires unsightly, in 1910 they were a source of civic pride and another sure-fire sign of progress. After all, the city was less than a year old when, on August 6, 1887, electric lights were turned on for the first time, and on the same date the *Daily News-Advertiser* became the first newspaper in Canada to be produced on electrically powered presses. Perhaps more important, in 1890, thanks to the foresight of Fire Chief Carlisle, Vancouver became the first city in North America to install Gamewell automatic electric fire-alarm boxes on its streets. Not all wires were power lines, of course; some were telephone lines. Again, progress came early to Vancouver. By the end of 1885 there were already thirty-five subscribers in Granville, the village that, a year later, was to become Vancouver. They were served by the New Westminster and Port Moody Telephone Company, a predecessor of BC Tel.

And what of those streetcars making their way up and down Granville Street? While stables were built on the assumption that the cars would be horse-drawn, the promoters and owners of the street railway system wisely decided that the coming thing was the electrically powered streetcar. The order for horse cars was cancelled and orders for electric streetcars were placed. When they went into service on June 26, 1890, the only other cities in North America that had electric lines were Detroit, Windsor, and Victoria.

"Progress" was a magic word in Vancouver before the First World War. In fact, the forerunner of the city's board of trade was the Progress Club. Growth and progress were seen as synonymous, and the club's motto was "Promoting Provincial Prosperity." It was a club much given to catchy slogans, and its banner, strung across Hastings Street in 1905, boldly proclaimed: "Many Men Making Money Means Much For Vancouver." While in 1910 progress may have seemed inevitable, a world-wide depression in 1912-13 and a world war between 1914 and 1918 put the idea of the inevitability of progress to rest for all time.

THE QUEEN VICTORIA MEMORIAL

Vancouver could never claim to be a city famous for commemorative sculpture. Nevertheless, what little there is has a certain appeal. The city's earliest monument is the Queen Victoria Memorial in Stanley Park. The memorial took the form of a drinking fountain flanked by curved stone seats. A place to get a drink of water and to sit for a minute or two wasn't a bad idea, as anyone who has "done" Stanley Park will agree. However, it isn't well situated, and many Vancouverites are unaware of its existence. As it is located far from any pedestrian walkway, visitors can only reach the fountain by skirting the perimeter road near the main park entrance. The memorial is across the road, not far beyond the harbourside Vancouver Rowing Club.

After Queen Victoria's death it was decided that the city's 4,669 school children should raise money for a monument. The youngsters were put to work selling specially printed black-edged memorial cards that recorded the dates of the Queen's birth, coronation, and death. These cards sold for ten cents each. Unfortunately, more money was needed, so in 1902 a gala patriotic concert was held to top off the fund.

While the names of the artists who created the various parts of the monument are known, the originator of the total concept is not. The stonework was produced in the yards of J. McIntosh and Sons at Westminster Avenue and Dufferin Street (now Main and Second), and the material used was Nelson Island granite. The bronze castings were designed by James Bloomfield and cast in England. The central portion of the casting incorporates a copy of a familiar portrait cameo of the Queen's head – an image which was used for the 1897 Diamond Jubilee medals and medallions.

James Bloomfield was a son of Henry Bloomfield, whose highly successful local firm specialized in the creation of artistic stained glass. James had studied architecture in his youth in England. Later, after his family settled in Vancouver, he went to Chicago and Europe to learn how to work in stained glass. In addition to creating the bronze-work designs for the Queen Victoria Memorial, James was responsible for creating Vancouver's coat of arms in 1903.

Like other drinking fountains of the day, the Queen Victoria Memorial was originally equipped with a pair of chained bronze drinking cups. Clearly, sanitation wasn't a great concern in those days. The inscription above the fountain reads, "IN MEMORY OF VICTORIA THE GOOD THIS MONUMENT IS ERECTED BY THE SCHOOL CHILDREN OF VANCOUVER, 1905." Appropriately, in the presence of the city's school children, the premier, Sir Richard McBride, unveiled the memorial in 1906 on the Queen's birthday, the twenty-fourth of May, and, doubtless to everyone's satisfaction, drank the official first cup of water!

"SOCIETY"

Gilbert and Sullivan's *Gondoliers* has a line that says, in effect, "When everybody is somebody then nobody is anybody." In all their light operas Gilbert and Sullivan devoted much of their time to spoofing social convention and pretention. One wonders what they might have done with a small book published in 1908 entitled *The Elite Directory of Vancouver*.

Its Foreword states: "Vancouver is growing so rapidly that every season makes more imperative the need for something in the nature of a Blue Book which shall be ... a reliable and complete roster ... of all persons properly recognized as constituting society. It is with pleasure therefore, that we offer to the Society people of Vancouver this unique book, relying with confidence upon the appreciation of the discriminating." The name, address, and afternoon when each of the "discriminating" families will be "At Home" comprises the bulk of the text. It is wonderful that the compilers could be absolutely certain that their roster contained the names of *all* persons constituting society!

The Elite Directory of Vancouver was not without advertising. Naturally, only those businesses acceptable to "Society" were allowed to appear in its pages. It was good to be able to read, for example, that the Imperial Roller Rink at English Bay was both "high class" and "refined." This assurance would doubtless have been a comfort to anxious "Ladies of Society."

One advertisement was for the Cabin Cafe at 691 West Hastings. In our picture, its oval sign can be seen in the middle of the block, half way between Seymour and Granville. It was located in the basement of the Davis Chambers, a five-storey office building designed by Daulton and Eveleigh in the latest Edwardian commercial style and built, in 1906, for E.P. Davis, the city's leading lawyer. Not surprisingly, the building's architects were among its tenants.

The Cabin Cafe's advertisement invited patrons "down the marble stairs for a Three Course Lunch or Afternoon Tea." The fact that very few cabins have, or ever had, marble stairs obviously didn't bother Lambert and Turner, the proprietors, one little bit. The Cabin featured a "Separate Ladies' Lunch Room," "Ladies' Toilet," and a "Ladies' Parlour," all of which tempt today's reader to think of the "Ladies of Society" as people with bodies so frail they had to rest after an arduous afternoon's shopping up the block at Birks (formerly Trorey's Jewellers) and with ears so delicate they could not bear to hear the things that might be said in a mixed dining room!

ALL HALLOWS, YALE

The story of All Hallows Girls' School at Yale began with the Right Reverend Acton Sillitoe, the first Anglican bishop of New Westminster. Soon after arriving in the diocese in 1879 he established two schools for girls, neither of which was self-supporting. Then in October, 1884, at his invitation, three Anglican nuns arrived at Yale from Ditchingham, England, to operate a day school for Native girls. The bishop told his diocese that, if schools for Native children were opened, then "we shall have wrought a social revolution in the land, for we shall have elevated the people from the servile condition of hewers of wood and drawers of water and given them an equal chance in the race of life."

Since the Native girls could not get to a day school on a regular basis, the sisters recommended the establishment of a Native girls' boarding school. As usual, Bishop Sillitoe was long on enthusiasm but short on cash. He did come up with an answer, though. He told the sisters that if they would take White boarders alongside Native girls, then money provided by an English missionary society could be used at Yale. Given the absence of alternatives, and the fact that the nuns had so little money that they had to take in washing to make ends meet, they went along with the plan. A large house was purchased for the school. It had belonged to Andrew Onderdonk, the contractor who had built the CPR line from Eagle Pass to Port Moody.

Even though he had already been turned down once, the bishop turned to the Department of Indian Affairs for additional financial help. He had more success on his second try. In June of 1888 an agreement was signed whereby the federal government would subsidize up to twenty-five pupils and fund the construction of a dormitory (which was built behind the Onderdonk house). The school was, for some time, a success. There were eventually thirty-five Native and forty-five White pupils enrolled, the latter being for the most part daughters of Lower Mainland families.

Changing White attitudes towards Native pupils, and better opportunities for private-school education for White girls closer to home, brought about the eventual closure of All Hallows. Government policy reflected popular public opinion when, in 1897, the minister responsible for Indian Affairs said that "we are educating these Indians to compete industrially with our own people, which seems to me to be a very undesirable use of public money ... The Indian cannot go out from school, making his own way ... and compete with the white man ... He has not the physical, mental or moral get-up to enable him to compete." Regarding the education of Native girls in 1910, it was said that education made "the girls ... too smart for the Indian villages." Times and attitudes had changed dramatically since the bishop had brought All Hallows into being.

In 1917 the recently established residential school for Native boys at Lytton offered to accommodate All Hallows' Native girls. The sisters gratefully accepted the invitation and closed their school in 1918. The White school closed in 1920, and, after thirty-six years, the sisters returned to England.

TRAINS TO ABBOTSFORD

Abbotsford townsite was laid out in 1889 by John Maclure, a former Royal Engineer and local homesteader. He named the new community after Henry Abbott, General Superintendent of the Pacific Division of the CPR, who was a brother of the prime minister, Sir John Abbott. The name was appropriate, since the town that came into being did so principally because the CPR had announced its intention to build a branch line from Mission to Huntingdon on the American border.

As it happened, everybody's railroad seemed to pass through Abbotsford! Our early 1910 picture of the main street looking west shows the presence of three rail lines. In the middle distance are flatcars loaded with lumber. They are on the CPR track that connected at the border with both the Bellingham Bay and British Columbia Railway (later a part of the Milwaukee Road) and with the Seattle, Lake Shore, and Eastern Railway (later a component of the Northern Pacific Railway).

In the far distance is a trestle and trackage belonging to the Great Northern Railway, which had opened its line between Abbotsford and Cloverdale in 1908. At Cloverdale passengers changed trains to go either to New Westminster and Vancouver or to Seattle. The third railway to make its way into Abbotsford was the BC Electric's line, which reached the town in January of 1910. The BC Electric track is in the foreground of the photograph. Full interurban passenger and freight service got under way in the fall of 1910. The town had one more railway to come. In August of 1913 the Northern Pacific acquired running rights over the Great Northern track from Huntingdon through Abbotsford to Vancouver.

Before the First World War, logging and lumbering were the major economic influences in the area. After the war, however, things changed. Agriculture began to replace logging, and by 1924, when the shallow Sumas Lake was drained and over 33,000 acres of farmland reclaimed, the economic picture had altered radically: Abbotsford was becoming the centre of a thriving dairy industry.

For all practical purposes, the heyday of railroading on the south side of the Fraser was over by the early 1930s. The CPR had discontinued its passenger service to Bellingham and Seattle via Abbotsford and Sumas in 1916. The Great Northern closed its Abbotsford station in August of 1929, and the rails were torn up in 1932, after the Northern Pacific gave up its running rights over Great Northern's tracks. The BC Electric's line was the last to offer passenger service, and it was discontinued on October 11, 1950.

But life goes on, and even though Abbotsford originally owed its existence to its strategic location "along the right of way," it has not only survived the end of the railroad era, it has become a thriving and vital city. Perhaps one of the special ironies is that what was the Great Northern's right of way is now the South Fraser Highway, the "main street" that runs through much of the new and growing Abbotsford.

HYCROFT

Shaughnessy Heights was laid out and landscaped for the CPR in 1907. The railway had successfully marketed its prestigious West End real estate twenty years before, and now it was time to introduce an opportunity for the city's elite to "move up" to Shaughnessy Heights.

The area was a veritable builder's catalogue of Edwardian architectural taste. As one of the newspapers of the day put it, "There is almost every style of residential architecture known to mankind ... in the array of fine buildings which cover Shaughnessy Heights." There is Scottish Baronial, Queen Anne, Southern Colonial, Spanish Mission, and that over-all favourite, English Tudor. All these Shaughnessy homes, regardless of style, had one thing in common: they created magnificent settings for entertaining. They also, of course, were intended to say something about the financial success, social prominence, and unerring good taste of the people who built them.

None shouted the message more loudly than Hycroft, the Italianate villa built between 1909 and 1911 for A.D. McRae. Born in Ontario in 1874, McRae made a respectable amount of money in Minnesota before the turn of the century. He then returned to Canada and built a fortune through investing in the Saskatchewan Valley Land Company, which he organized and controlled. The company made over nine million dollars in the Prairie land settlement boom. His involvement with Canadian Western Lumber brought him to Vancouver in 1907, and he then went on to national prominence. During the First World War he became first the quarter-master general of all Canadian forces and then a major-general and head of the Ministry of Information under Lord Beaverbrook. After the war, he became a Conservative MP, and, ultimately, when he lost his Commons seat, he was made a senator.

Hycroft had a magnificent site that provided a commanding view of the city before trees grew tall and neighbouring apartments grew even taller. Even though the name of the architect is still uncertain, the McRae house was indeed grand. In 1912 the *Vancouver Daily Province* reported: "The residence is laid out in a most elaborate manner ... House and furnishings represent an expenditure of more the $250,000 ... the world was ransacked for the decorations and furnishings ...The house is the most conspicuous in Shaughnessy Heights." Even though it is very much an Edwardian pastiche of styles – Grecian Corinthian columns, Italian tiled roof, English panelling and scenic wallpapers – no one could argue with that last statement. The sheer size of Hycroft along with its complement of outbuildings – stable, carriage house, and servants' quarters – made it an impressive sight.

Again, to quote local newspapers: "The Shaughnessy mansions make a most pleasing sight to automobile parties as they drive along the smooth pavements and superb roads that have been built simultaneously with the houses." People still "automobile" through Shaughnessy, and Hycroft is probably still the home that forms the greatest and most lasting impression. While its stables and carriage house have been torn down, the house is now the beautifully maintained home of the University Women's Club.

BRIGHTON OR BLACKPOOL YES, BUT...

Brighton or Blackpool yes, but a promenade pier at English Bay? Why? one might ask. Most likely it was because Vancouver's many English-born residents wanted a pier. They would have retained fond memories of the piers at Brighton, Blackpool, or any one of the many seaside resorts they left behind in the "Old Country." Whatever the reason, on January 24, 1907, the Vancouver Parks Board instructed J. E. Parr (of Parr and Fee, the prestigious Vancouver architectural firm that was responsible for the design of many West End homes) to prepare plans for a promenade pier and landing stage at English Bay.

Parr's plan was approved, and on May 8, 1907, the BC General Contracting Company's bid of $21,000 was accepted and the firm authorized to begin construction. At the same time the federal government was asked for the necessary permission to build the pier, which, of course, would reach out far beyond the high-tide mark. Permission was granted. The new pier was completed prior to the November 13, 1907, meeting of the Parks Board. Perhaps plans had been completed too hastily, but, at any rate, at its next meeting the Parks Board had to ask Parr to prepare plans for both "refreshment rooms" and "toilet rooms" at the new pier, at a cost not to exceed $1,500. Plans changed again in February 1908, when it was agreed that the "outdoor platform" adjacent to the tea room should be larger. The Parks Board agreed to pay an additional $300 for the bigger platform. Motivated by either a spirit of generosity or a good understanding of public relations, the BC Electric announced that it would pay the $750 it would cost to install ornamental cluster lights on the pier. Furthermore, the company offered to charge a flat rate of only a dollar per night for the necessary electricity.

The Tea and Refreshment Parlour was leased to C.N. Lee, who had submitted the highest bid. Lee agreed to pay $375 per year for the first two years of a five-year lease and $475 per year for each of the remaining three years. Lee was also expected to accept responsibility for turning the electric lights on at dusk and for turning them off at ten-thirty in the evening. The boating facilities were leased for $1,500 a year for five years. Quite obviously, there was more money to be made in boat rentals than in serving afternoon tea!

The pier had a relatively short life – a mere thirty-two years. It was torn down in 1939, as wood rot and years of neglect had made it unsafe. The pier was located between Gilford and Chilco Streets off Beach Avenue. At low tide a line of stones – all that remains of the pier's foundations – can still be seen stretching out into English Bay. Those who remember just how enjoyable a walk on the pier could be will possibly wonder why the powers that be have never seen fit to replace such a pleasurable and popular waterfront amenity.

The First Bridge At New Westminster

A procession of steamers, a civic luncheon, Native canoe races, a torchlight procession on the river, and fireworks were all part of New Westminster's celebrations on July 23, 1904. And what was the occasion? Lieutenant-Governor Sir Henri-Gustave Joly de Lotbinière's opening of the New Westminster Bridge across the Fraser River. The opening took place in the presence of a host of dignitaries, including the local MLA, Richard McBride, who also happened to be premier of British Columbia.

The new million-dollar bridge not only benefited New Westminster, but also the entire south side of the Fraser Valley. No longer would people have to make the slow crossing from South Westminster on the old ferry, *Surrey*. Perhaps more important, the bridge meant that rail lines could be run through New Westminster to Vancouver. McBride was an enthusiastic supporter of railway construction, and his active interest doubtless did much to ensure that the bridge was built.

The bridge had two decks: the upper level was designed to carry wagons and motor vehicles, while the lower level was designed for rail traffic. Within a few years the BC Electric (now Southern Railway of BC), the Canadian Northern Railway (now part of CN Rail), the Great Northern Railway (now Burlington Northern Railway), and the CPR were all using the New Westminster Bridge.

The new bridge was no doubt regarded by local residents as being at least as significant as any one of the Seven Wonders of the Ancient World. And it *was* impressive. Not only had it cost over a million dollars to build, but it crossed a 2,200-foot expanse of water. When they were put in place, its piers were claimed to be the second deepest in the world, some being 141 feet below the high-water mark and extending sixty-nine feet into the river bed. The pivot pier for the swing span was driven ninety feet into the clay below the river. The sub-structure and approaches were the work of a Vancouver firm, Armstrong, Morrison and Balfour, and the superstructure was built by the Dominion Bridge Company of Montreal. As construction seems to be fairly well advanced in our picture, the photo probably dates from late 1903.

Motor traffic stopped using the bridge on November 15, 1937, when the Pattullo Bridge was opened. Even though it was no longer needed for vehicular traffic, the old bridge continued to be an important Lower Mainland transportation link. In 1992 CN Rail spent fifteen million dollars upgrading the bridge, and some fifty trains a day (85 per cent of which belong to CN Rail) still use the crossing. The span is opened, on average, around seventeen times a day to allow the passage of marine traffic. It would be hard to argue that the million dollars spent building the New Westminster Bridge ninety years ago wasn't money well spent.

CPR Depot and Docks

Those of us who were in school in the 1920s, '30s, or '40s may remember getting free dust jackets in September for our new text books. These brown paper covers were given away as advertising by banks and other firms. We cut and glued these paper jackets so our books would still be "as new" when we went to sell them at the end of the school year. One of the cover designs featured an art deco montage showing a speeding streamline train, an obviously fast and luxurious ocean liner, a stylized automobile, and, in the sky, a biplane off to heaven knows where. Our picture of the CPR's depot and docks circa 1910 or 1911 is, minus the biplane, a real-life version of the dust-jacket picture.

It's the beginning of a busy morning at the train station. The daily *Imperial Limited* is scheduled to arrive from Montreal at eight-twenty-five and the *Toronto Express* leaves for the east at nine o'clock. It is close enough to the first arrival that the hotel buses are already lined up and waiting to the left of Edward Maxwell's wonderful 1899 brick and stone station. At least half the buses awaiting the influx of travellers appear to be motor-driven. Those tourists with reservations at Glencoe Lodge at Georgia and Burrard will ignore these buses, as they have been advised to take a taxi, at the lodge's expense. Such instructions were in keeping with the Glencoe's self image as "the leading high class family Hotel of Vancouver."

To the right of the station, the *Charmer* is just arriving from Victoria, while the *Princess Charlotte,* already arrived from Seattle, sits at dock. Built in 1887 in San Francisco for the Canadian Pacific Navigation Company (which was bought out by the CPR in 1901 to enable the railway to enter the coastal trade), the *Charmer* was 200 feet long and had an iron hull. It was the first vessel on the British Columbia coast to be equipped with electric lights.

Two trans-Pacific liners are docked at the CPR's pier, which was built in 1900. An *Empress* is moored on the east side of the wharf. Whether it is the *Empress of Japan, China,* or *India* it is impossible to say, as the ships were virtually identical, with only their respective figureheads being unique. The other large ship docked on the west side of the pier belongs to the Union Steamship Company of New Zealand. This line provided a monthly service between Vancouver, Australia, and New Zealand, with stops at Hawaii and, later, Fiji.

Riding at anchor is a four-masted lumber schooner. While they were becoming a thing of the past, sailing ships remained a relatively common sight in Vancouver's harbour until well into the 1920s. If one looks carefully, shacks can be seen along the waterfront in Stanley Park. It wasn't until 1926 that the squatters who lived along the shore off Brockton Point were evicted.

NEW WESTMINSTER'S COLUMBIAN COLLEGE

In January 1881, the Methodists opened a collegiate institute or high school in the basement of their church in New Westminster. This first local foray into the field of education lasted only two years before the school was merged with the city's high school. The denomination's interest in higher education continued, however, and in 1892 the BC Conference of the Methodist Church opened Columbian College in rented buildings on Ash Street in the Royal City.

The provincial legislature incorporated Columbian Methodist College in 1893, thereby making it the first institution of higher learning in British Columbia. Initially, the college offered senior high-school programs and, in affiliation with the University of Toronto, the first two years of an Arts program. As early as 1903, Columbian College was actively anticipating the day when it would be offering a full four-year course that would qualify candidates for a University of Toronto BA. The institution, however, never really got to be much more than a junior college. It offered a commercial course, teacher training, piano, and what at the time was called "voice culture." A 1903 article in the *British Columbian* proudly announced that the school offered "an excellent ladies' college course leading to the degrees of M.E.L. and M.L.A." "MEL" stood for "Mistress of English Literature" and was a one-year diploma course; "MLA" stood for "Mistress of Liberal Arts" and was a two-year diploma course. The only degrees actually conferred by Columbian College were those awarded to men who successfully completed a course in theological studies in order to qualify for the Methodist ministry. Even though Columbian College was a Methodist school, denominationalism was never stressed. All students, though, were obliged to attend at least one Sunday service a week in the church of their parents' choice.

The college moved from its rented buildings in 1893, when it purchased Blossom Grove, Henry Edmonds's estate at First and Queens – a purchase made possible by local donations and generous gifts from Toronto's Massey family. This large Victorian home had been designed by G.W. Grant, an architect of some prominence. Among his later creations were New Westminster's court house and Vancouver's Carnegie Library. Gradually, new buildings, including a men's residence, junior classrooms, and a gymnasium, were added to the college. Typically, the gym was funded largely through the efforts of students and alumni. The Ladies' Residence (pictured) was the original Edmonds home, remodelled and enlarged.

A number of factors led to the closure of Columbian College. To be near the new University of British Columbia, Methodist theological education was moved to the new Ryerson Methodist College in Vancouver in 1923. For the last ten years of its existence, Columbian College was essentially a residential high school offering academic senior matriculation courses. Finally, in 1936 the Depression forced the college to close. Its site was sold, its buildings razed, and its grounds subdivided. All that remains are memories.

SQUAMISH

While Europeans had passed through the Squamish Valley as early as 1858, the year of the Cariboo Gold Rush, real settlement didn't take place until much later. Even the building of a narrow road from Lillooet to Lynn Creek at a cost of $38,000 in 1873 had no effect on settlement. The route was just too rough and dangerous to be practical, and it was abandoned after one year.

In 1885 a party of Norwegians settled at the head of Howe Sound in the Squamish Valley, but when floods swept away their homes they moved on to Bella Coola. The first people to come and stay were settlers from Manitoba, who arrived in 1888. They were soon joined by families from Ontario. While farming was initially the principal source of income, it wasn't too many years before logging became important in the Squamish Valley.

It is impossible to say anything about the history of Squamish without talking about two companies: the Union Steamship Company and the Pacific Great Eastern (PGE) Railway. The Union Steamship Company first provided regular scheduled service to the town on July 12, 1891. The *Skidegate* sailed each Monday at 8:00 AM from Vancouver to Squamish River, stopping en route at other small Howe Sound communities. Union Steamship vessels remained an important part of Squamish life until the completion of the PGE from Vancouver to Squamish in 1956. While as early as 1891 there had been talk of building a railroad from Vancouver, over the Coast Range, and on through the Cariboo, it wasn't until 1910 that the first line actually opened – ten miles of track going from Squamish to Cheekeye, which was built by the Howe Sound, Pemberton Valley and Northern Railway. In 1912 the provincial government chose the PGE as the company to build a railway from North Vancouver to Prince George, where it would connect with the Grand Trunk Pacific. After acquiring the ten miles of existing track, opening a line from North Vancouver to Horseshoe Bay on June 1, 1914, and laying track from Cheekeye to Clinton by December 1915, work was halted because of lack of money. In August 1918 the provincial government assumed control of the company, and the railway reached Quesnel in 1921. Quesnel remained the end of the line until 1952, when track finally went through to Prince George. The North Vancouver-Horseshoe Bay portion of the line, which had been abandoned in 1928, was rebuilt and continued on to Squamish in 1956. On April 1, 1972, the PGE became the British Columbia Railway.

During much of its history, Squamish has had a special appeal for both steamship fans and train buffs. It would have been worth the trip to Squamish just to be able to walk the 800-foot wharf shown in our picture! Today, however, it is no longer just a quaint town at one end of a railway "going from nowhere to nowhere" but an important commercial and residential centre that is home to an ever-increasing number of people who commute daily to Vancouver. Wharf or no wharf, thousands of train lovers still travel to Squamish annually on one of BC's greatest travel adventures – the Royal Hudson, with its steam engine and vintage passenger coaches.

"Birks" Clock

Vancouver's downtown shopping streets were a pleasant place to be. Shops, shaded by colourful awnings that protected the inviting and elaborate window displays, lined the streets. Pictured is Granville and Hastings at eleven-fifteen on a sunny spring morning in 1906. How do we know it was eleven-fifteen? Because the clock on the corner says so.

The clock belonged to George E. Trorey, Vancouver's premier jeweller and watchmaker. The thirty-three-year-old Trorey had come to Vancouver from Niagara Falls, Ontario, in 1893 to open a jewelery store. His business at 102 East Cordova did so well that, in 1900, he opened a second store in the new Haddon Building on the northeast corner of Granville and Hastings. Within a year he closed his shop on Cordova, which was no longer a particularly good address for a fashionable jeweller. Trorey's reputation was such that the CPR chose him to be its official watch inspector. He employed as many as ten watch-makers at any one time.

George Trorey had many interests. He was a founder of the Vancouver Tourist Association and first president of the Vancouver Bicycle Club. Nevertheless, his chief interest was in watches and clocks. To mark his fifth year at Granville and Hastings, Trorey requested and received civic permission to place a clock on the curb, where it could be seen by passers-by on either street.

The clock was made on special order by E. Howard and Company of Boston, Massachusetts. It was to be of ornamental iron, approximately twenty feet high, and its four dials (which could be electrically illuminated at night) were to be three feet in diameter. It was to cost something less than $2,000. Its makers guaranteed that it would keep the correct time to within two seconds per day. While the clock was, and still is, wound with a key once a week, it was fitted with a small electric heating unit to offset dampness. E. Howard and Company would have known all about coastal climate and the chilling dampness that goes right through both people and clocks alike!

Because Harvey Haddon was having some work done on his building, the new clock could not be put in place when it was delivered in November 1905, and its unveiling had to wait until February 1906. As it happened, Trorey sold out to Henry Birks and Sons of Montreal in the same year. Thereafter, in the public mind, the clock became firmly associated with Birks. The firm moved the clock to the corner of Granville and Georgia in time for the grand opening of its new store on November 10, 1913.

When Birks relocated to the southeast corner of Granville and Hastings in November 1994, the famous clock moved yet again. Birks Clock now stands less than a hundred feet from where George Trorey had it placed back in 1906.

THE HUDSON'S BAY COMPANY

In 1887 the Hudson's Bay Company opened what it aptly called "an unpretentious store" in Vancouver. It was on Cordova Street and was limited to selling groceries, provisions, and wine and spirits – those things prospectors, trappers, and loggers would most appreciate both before and after they headed up the Coast or into the Interior. In 1890 the company opened a branch store on Granville, a street that was becoming an attractive address for fashionable retailers. Business boomed and it soon became obvious that larger and more suitable premises were needed. Property at Granville and Georgia, the site of the present store, was purchased, and a four-storey brick and stone building was erected. At its opening on September 21, 1893, only two of its four floors were needed. By 1897, however, the whole building was occupied by what the company described as "a business with many departments."

The available space was more than doubled in the spring of 1899, when the store received a much-needed addition. The accompanying picture shows the building as it was from 1899 to 1905. To create still more space the building was further enlarged in 1905, and the wine and liquor department moved across the street to the Strathcona Block (the building that occupied the southeast corner before Birks Jewellers bought the site). By 1905 the Hudson's Bay Company store featured eighteen different retail departments. The company employed 150 people, and proudly advertised that "an unexcelled delivery service is maintained with twelve teams in commission."

By 1910 still more space was needed. It was wisely decided that nothing could be done with the rather unprepossessing structure that housed the firm, and on July 20, 1912, it was announced that a new two-million dollar building would replace the existing one. The press release of July 20, 1912, spoke of a ten-storey fireproof building facing on to Georgia Street and extending from Granville to Seymour. The architects were to be Burke, Horwood and White of Toronto, who had earlier designed the company's Calgary store. It was in Calgary that they first presented what would become almost a Hudson's Bay Company trademark – grey-white terracotta facing, graceful Corinthian columns, and ornamental lighting at precise intervals along the rooftop parapet.

Since the new store was to be built in two phases – the Georgia and Seymour half first, the Georgia and Granville half second – so as not to dislocate business any more than was necessary, the brick and stone structure was not torn down until the mid-1920s, when the second portion of the new store was built.

BIBLIOGRAPHY

Books and Periodicals

A Centennial Commentary Upon The Early Days of Squamish, B.C., Squamish, B.C., Squamish Centennial Committee, 1958.

Adolph, Val, *Woodlands – 100 Years of Progress,* New Westminster, self published, 1978.

Allen, Richard Edward, *A Pictorial History of Vancouver, Book 1, Origin of Street and Place Names,* Vancouver, self published, 1982.

Barman, Jean, "Separate and Unequal: Indian and White Girls at All Hallows School, 1884–1920, " *Indian Education in Canada (Volume 1),* Vancouver, B.C., University of British Columbia Press, 1986.

Barr, Capt. James, *Ferry Across the Harbor,* Vancouver, B.C., Mitchell Press Limited, 1969.

Barrett, Anthony A. & Liscombe, Rhodri Windsor, *Francis Rattenbury and British Columbia: Architecture and Challenge in the Imperial Age,* Vancouver, B.C., University of British Columbia Press, 1983.

Bingham, Janet, *Samuel Maclure – Architect,* Ganges, B.C., Horsdal & Shubart, 1985.

Boam, Henry J., with Brown, Ashley G., *British Columbia,* London, England, Sells Ltd., 1912.

Bohi, Charles, *Canadian National's Western Depots,* Toronto, Ontario, Railfare Enterprises Limited, 1977.

Breen David & Coates Kenneth, *The Pacific National Exhibition – An Illustrated History,* Vancouver, B.C., University of British Columbia Press, 1982.

Burdick, J.R., Ed., *Pioneer Post Cards,* New York, N.Y., Nostalgia Press, undated.

Burnes, J. Rodger, *Echoes of the Ferries,* North Vancouver, B.C., self published, (1974).

Burnes, John Roger, *North Vancouver, 1891-1907,* North Vancouver, B.C., self published, (1971).

Burrows, Roger G., *Railway Mileposts: British Columbia (Volume 1: The CPR Mainline Route: From the Rockies to the Pacific,)* North Vancouver, B.C., Railway Milepost Books, 1981.

Burrows, Roger G., *Railway Mileposts: British Columbia (Volume 2: The Southern Routes From The Crowsnest to the Coquihalla,)* North Vancouver, B.C., Railway Milepost Books, 1984.

Cheerington, John, *Mission on the Fraser,* Vancouver, B.C., Mitchell Press, 1974.

Coutts, Cecil C., *Cancelled With Pride,* Chilliwack, B.C., Cecil C. Coutts Publishing, 1993.

Davis, Chuck, *The Vancouver Book,* North Vancouver, B.C., J.J. Douglas Ltd., 1976.

Downs, Art, *Paddlewheels On The Frontier,* Seattle, Washington, Superior Publishing Company, 1972.

Drushka, *Against Wind and Weather: The History of Towboating in British Columbia,* Vancouver, B.C., Douglas & McIntyre, 1981.

Duval, William with Monahan, Valerie, *Collecting Postcards in Colour, 1898–1914,* England, Blandford Press, 1978.

Ewert, Henry, *The Story of the B.C. Electric Railway Company,* North Vancouver, B.C., Whitecap Books Ltd., 1986.

Fanelli, Giovanni & Godoli, *Art Nouveau Postcards,* New York, N.Y., Rizzoli, 1987.

Forester, Joseph E., & Anne D., *Fishing – British Columbia's Commercial Fishing History,* Sannichton, B.C., Hancock House Publishers Ltd., 1975.

Gosnell, R.E., *The Year Book of British Columbia and Manual of Provincial Information,* Victoria, B.C., The Government of the Province of British Columbia, (Coronation Edition) 1911.

Hacking, Norman R., and W. Kaye Lamb, *The Princess Story,* Vancouver, B.C., Mitchell Press Limited, 1974.

Hale, Linda, comp., *Vancouver Centennial Bibliography,* 4 Vols., Vancouver B.C., Vancouver Historical Society, 1986.

Horton, Timothy J., *The Pacific Great Eastern Railway (Volume One,)* Calgary, Alberta., B.R.M.N.A., 1986.

Howard, Irene, *Bowen Island, 1872–1972,* Bowen Island, B.C., Bowen Island Histories, 1973.

Howay, F.W., and Scholefield, E.O.S., *British Columbia From the Earliest Times to the Present: Biographical, Vols. 3 & 4,* Toronto, Ontario, S.J. Clarke Publishing Ltd., 1914.

Imready, Doreen, "Birks' Clock," *British Columbia Historical News*, Vol. 7, No. 3, April 1974.

Imready, Peggy, *Guide to Sculpture in Vancouver,* Vancouver, B.C., self published, 1980.

Kalman, Harold, *Exploring Vancouver,* Vancouver, B.C., The University of British Columbia Press, 1974.

Kearney, Jim, *Champions – A British Columbia Sports Album,* Vancouver, B.C., Douglas & McIntyre Ltd., 1985.

Kloppenborg, Anne, et al, *Vancouver's First Century,* Vancouver, B.C., J.J. Douglas Ltd., 1977.

Kluckner, Michael, *Vancouver – The Way It Was,* North Vancouver, B.C., Whitecap Books Ltd., 1984.

Kluckner, Michael, *Vanishing Vancouver,* North Vancouver, B.C., Whitecap Books Ltd., 1990.

Ladner, T.E., *Above the Sandheads,* self published, 1979.

Lamb, W. Kaye, *Empress To The Orient,* Vancouver, B.C., Vancouver Maritime Museum Society, 1991.

Lavallee, Omer, *Van Horne's Road,* Montreal, P.Q., Railfar Enterprises Limited, 1974.

Leonoff, Cyril E., *An Enterprising Life,* Vancouver, B.C., Talonbooks, 1990.

Macdonald, Bruce, *Vancouver – A Visual History,* Vancouver, B.C., Talonbooks, 1992.

McDonald, Robert A.J. & Barman, Jean, *Vancouver Past: Essays in Social History,* Vancouver, B.C., University of British Columbia Press, 1986.

McKee, William, *Portholes & Pilings,* Vancouver, B.C., City of Vancouver Archives, Occasional Paper Number 1, 1978.

Maiden, Cecil, *Lighted Journey – The Story of the B.C. Electric,* Vancouver, B.C., Public Information Department, BC Electric Co., Ltd., 1948.

Martin, J. Edward, *The Railway Stations of Western Canada,* White Rock, B.C., Studio E Martin, 1980.

Matches, Alex, *It Began With A Ronald,* Vancouver, B.C., Vancouver City Archives, 1932.

Matthews, J.S., *Early Vancouver: Narratives of Pioneers of Vancouver, B.C., Collected During 1931-1932,* Vancouver, B.C., Vancouver City Archives, 1932.

Melvin, George H., *The Post Offices of British Columbia, 1958 - 1970,* Vernon, B.C., self published, 1972.

Morton, J.W., *Capilano – The Story of a River,* Toronto, Ontario, McClelland and Stewart Limited, 1970.

Mount Pleasant Early Days – Memories of Reuben Hamilton Pioneer 1890, Vancouver, B.C., Vancouver City Archives, 1957.

Orchard, Imbert, *Floodland and Forest,* Sound Heritage Series, Number 37, Victoria, B.C., Provincial Archives of British Columbia, 1983.

Orchard, Imbert, *Growing Up In The Valley,* Sound Heritage Series Number 40, Victoria, B.C., Provincial Archives of British Columbia, 1983.

Patterson, T.W., *Lower Mainland,* Langley, B.C., B.C. Ghost Towns Series: 2, Sunfire Publications Ltd., 1984.

Reksten, Terry, *Rattenbury,* Victoria, B.C., Sono Nis Press, 1978.

Rendall, Belle, *Healing Waters,* Harrison Hot Springs, B.C., self published, 1974.

Roberts, Shelia, *Shakespeare in Vancouver, 1889–1918,* Vancouver, B.C., Vancouver Historical Society, Occasional Paper Number 3, 1971.

Robinson, J., Lewis & Hardwick, Walter G., *British Columbia One Hundred Years of Geographical Change,* Vancouver, B.C., Talonbooks, 1973.

Roy, Patrica E., *Vancouver – An Illustrated History,* Toronto, Ontario, James Lorimer & Company, Publishers, 1980.

Roy, Reginald H., *The Vancouver Club – First Century 1889-1989,* Vancouver, B.C., The Vancouver Club, 1989.

Rushton, Gerald A., *Whistle Up the Inlet,* Vancouver, B.C., J.J. Douglas Ltd., 1974.

Rushton, Gerald, *Echoes of the Whistle,* Vancouver, B.C., Douglas & McIntyre Ltd., 1980.

Sandison, James M. ed., *Schools of Old Vancouver,* Vancouver, B.C., Vancouver Historical Society, 1971.

Schooling, Sir William, K.B.E., *The Governor and Company of Adventurers of England Trading into Hudson's Bay during Two Hundred and Fifty Years – 1670–1920,* London, England, 1920.

Sleigh, Daphne, *The People of the Harrison,* Deroche, B.C., self published, 1990.

Squamish, Squamish, B.C., Squamish & Howe Sound Chamber of Commerce, 1989.

Steele, Richard (Mike) *The First 100 Years: An Illustrated Celebration,* Vancouver, B.C., The Vancouver Board of Parks and Recreation, 1988.

Steel, Richard M., *The Stanley Park Explorer,* North Vancouver, B.C., Whitecap Books Ltd., 1985.

Steinhart, Allan L., *The Postal History of the Post Card in Canada, 1878 - 1911,* Toronto, Ontario, self published, 1979.

Taylor, Geoffrey W., *Builders of British Columbia,* Victoria, B.C., Morriss Publishing, 1982.

Taylor, Geoffrey W., *The Automobile Saga of British Columbia, 1864–1914,* Victoria, B.C., Morriss Publishing, 1984.

Taylor, Geoffrey W., *Shipyards of British Columbia,* Victoria, B.C., Morriss Publishing, 1986.

Taylor, Geoffrey W., *The Railway Contractors,* Victoria, B.C., Morriss Publishing, 1988.

Turner, Robert D., *The Pacific Princesses,* Victoria, B.C., Sono Nis Press, 1977.

Turner, Robert D., *The Pacific Empresses,* Victoria, B.C., Sono Nis Press, 1981.

Turner, Robert D., *Sternwheelers and Steam Tugs,* Victoria, B.C., Sono Nis Press, 1984.

Turner, Robert, D., *West of the Great Divide,* Victoria, B.C., Sono Nis Press, 1987.

Vancouver Annual, Vancouver, B.C., Progress Club, 1912.

Waites, K.A., *The First Fifty Years – Vancouver Schools, 1890-1940,* Vancouver, B.C., Vancouver School Board, 1941.

Woods, J.J., *The Agassi – Harrison Valley,* Agassi, B.C., Kent Centennial Committee, 1941.

Woods, J.J. & Chittenden, W., *The Harrison-Chehalis Challenge,* Harrison Hot Springs, B.C., Treeline Publishing, 1988.

Working Lives – Vancouver 1886-1986, Vancouver, B.C., New Star Books, 1985.

Newspapers & Periodicals

BC Studies.

Chilliwack Progress.

New Westminster Columbian.

Royal City Record.

Urban Reader.

Vancouver History.

Vancouver New-Advertiser.

Vancouver Daily Province.

Vancouver Sun.

Vancouver World.

INDEX

About the Authors

Fred Thirkell and Bob Scullion bring wide and varied experience to their cooperative ventures. While Fred was born in Vancouver, where he attended local schools and UBC, Bob is a native of Glasgow, where his education included an apprenticeship with one of the city's shipbuilders.

Fred's almost life-long enthusiasm for collecting postcards, particularly those relating to Vancouver and the Fraser Valley before the First World War, reflects his keen interest in local history. He has served on the boards of the Vancouver Museum and Planetarium Association and the Vancouver Maritime Museum. He is currently president of the Friends of the City of Vancouver Archives.

In his youth, Bob was a participant in the first Outward Bound Program for older apprentices at the Moray Sea School in the North of Scotland. He played semi-professional soccer in Glasgow and coached juvenile soccer after coming to Canada. Bob lawn bowled for Canada in the 1990 Commonwealth Games in New Zealand and has played in numerous overseas invitational tournaments. He has even tried to teach Fred to lawn bowl!

Having grown up in Glasgow, Britain's best preserved Victorian city, Bob shares Fred's appreciation of cities and their history. Together they develop concepts, design, and content for calendars (along with other publications) under the name of Canadian Historical Calendars.Fred and Bob are currently working on a second book for Heritage House, *Places Remembered.*